The RYA Book of
Race
Training

Other titles in the series

The RYA Book of Navigation: Tim Bartlett
ISBN 0 7136 4409 5

The RYA Book of Navigation is *the* reference text for anyone following RYA
navigation courses, from Day Skipper through to Yachtmaster Offshore.
Covering the latest examination syllabuses the author explains how to read
and understand charts and then takes the reader logically through the stages
of navigation: measuring direction and distance; electronic equipment;
position fixing; tides; the difference between dead reckoning and estimated
position; lights, buoys and fog signals; radar; pilotage; and finally passage-
making. By the end of the book readers should be fully conversant with what
it takes to navigate a yacht or motorboat safely and accurately.

The RYA Book of
Race Training

Third Edition

Jim Saltonstall

ADLARD COLES NAUTICAL
London

Third Edition 1996
Published by Adlard Coles Nautical
an imprint of A & C Black (Publishers) Ltd
35 Bedford Row, London WC1R 4JH

Copyright © Jim Saltonstall 1983, 1990, 1996

First edition published as *RYA Race Training Manual*
by William Heinemann Ltd, 1983
Second edition published by Macmillan Press Ltd 1990
Third edition published as *The RYA Book of Race
Training* by Adlard Coles Nautical 1996

ISBN 0–7136–4284–X

A CIP catalogue record for this book is available from
the British Library.

Typeset in 10/12 pt Concorde by Falcon Oast Graphic Art
Printed and bound in Hong Kong by
Wing King Tong Co Ltd

Acknowledgements

I would like to offer my sincere thanks to the following people for all their help in producing this book: First, my wife Christine for all the hard work and hours spent at the keyboard putting the project together; Dr Frank Newton and his wife Jeny for their valuable input on 'self preparation,' and also for their support – especially that given to the UK Youth Race Training Scheme; Roger and June Lean-Vercoe for the excellent photographs that are included in this book; and John Reed, RYA Racing Manager, for his support and encouragement during all the years we have worked together – and for writing the Foreword to the book. Finally, I would like to thank the IYRU for allowing the reproduction of some of the Racing Rules and Proctor Masts and Super Spars for allowing me to use their spar selection guides.

Contents

Foreword

We had been spectating at the 405 final – we being my 15-year-old son and myself – and were in the Parkstone Yacht Club. Me at the bar with a pint and son George in the audience for Jim Saltonstall's debriefing. We hadn't eaten since breakfast and so, feeling very hungry and expecting son to be chewing the buttons off the leather armchairs, I slid up to him and whispered, 'Come on George, let's go and get a MacDonald's'. He looked at me in amazement, 'What? And miss Jim's talk?'

Now the extraordinary thing about this is that normally, even after a four-course lunch, George would almost be prepared to leave home for a hamburger, and as for a MacDonald's – well, previous to this incident, I thought that there was nothing, but nothing, that would keep him from one. So that is the measure of Jim's charisma, his depth of knowledge, and his ability to communicate. That he can also coach and lead our British youth sailors is evidenced by the innumerable sailing gold medals won by past and present members of the RYA Youth Squad. In fact, a great deal of the credit for the successes of British sailors in international yacht racing is due to Jim.

However, not everyone can be in a team coached and managed by Jim, and not everyone can listen rapt as he lectures on tactics or boat speed, but you can read his book – and I can assure you that it is the next best thing. The accumulated knowledge and experience of one of the world's top youth sailing coaches is here, and his enthusiasm and inspiration makes it all absorbing reading.

For anyone seeking to improve their enjoyment and ability in the wonderful sport of yacht and dinghy racing, this book is definitely required reading.

John Reed
RYA Racing Manager

Introduction

If you want to be a future winner in the sport of sailing you will find a great deal of help within these pages – *so read on!*

There is no thrill like winning. In any walk of life, if you succeed in reaching the top you feel a great sense of achievement. However, this rarely happens without immense effort.

In the majority of sports, in order to win a major event you must have:

- Commitment
- Dedication
- Determination
- Controlled aggression
- Concentration
- Physical fitness
- Positive thinking
- Financial backing

OK, so it sounds impossible! Not so – many before you have succeeded, and you can too. And the good news is that you do not have to give up everything else in order to win a major championship. There can be – in fact, *must* be – a life beyond sailing, but you have to plan carefully. A person whose whole life is devoted to 'being on the water' can feel very insecure because at the back of their mind is always the question, 'What will I have if I can no longer sail?' It is important to balance the time needed for training and competing against your work, home and social life, and in that way you should have a more relaxed attitude to your racing – and you are also less likely to become 'burned out'.

Preparation

Nothing, though, is ever achieved without forward thinking, ie preparation; and this needs to be carried out thoroughly in all areas in order to succeed in your campaign to win.

Listed below are the main categories in which thorough preparation must be made:

1 **Championship preparation** – campaign, chartwork, training programme, measurement and travel.

2 **Self preparation** – physical and psychological.

3 **Boat preparation** – hull, spars, sails, foils and measurement.

4 **Boat handling** – each point of sailing (all conditions) and crew work.

5 **Boat tuning** – for all weather conditions and sea states.

6 **Race strategy** – which way to go, relating to land masses and tides.

7 **Starting** – how to achieve the best start position, line bias and gate starts.

8 **Tactics** – fleet and boat to boat (start, beat, reach, run).

9 **Racing rules** – definitions, Rules 31–46 applying on the race area, and protests.

10 **Compass work** – overall use from pre-start orientation to finish.

11 **Meteorology** – familiarity with local weather systems and daily forecasting.

For those of you wanting to become top class 'yachters', I have tried to give help and advice in all these categories. I really hope that you will find this information useful, and that it will help you to achieve your ambition.

Note: In any instance where 'he', 'him' and 'his' are used in this book 'she', 'her' and 'hers' can equally well be substituted. No preference is intended.

The 5 'P's = Poor Preparation Produces Poor Performance. Completing your Race Training Programme will prevent this from happening to you!

Championship Preparation

Preparation time for a championship event will vary, depending upon the type of boat being sailed. For example, the time necessary to prepare a campaign for the Whitbread Round the World Yacht Race cannot compare to the amount of time needed to get ready for a singlehanded dinghy world championship. Obviously I'm using two extremes as an example here, but all the categories of preparation listed in the Introduction apply to both situations. In other words, whatever class of boat you sail, you must allow sufficient time for preparation if you intend to win.

Campaign

Once you have checked the date and venue of the championship you wish to enter, the following points all become vitally important:

1 **Acquire a chart** of the race area. This, of course, applies more to a championship that is to be held on the open sea.

2 Find out the **closing date** for entries, and make sure that yours is sent off in good time.

3 **Establish a training programme** for yourself and any crew members.

4 **Confirm all travel plans** and **check all tickets**.

5 **Check passports, visas and international driver's licence**, where necessary, and make sure that they are all valid.

6 If **inoculations** are necessary, make sure that these are done in good time.

7 Make sure that your **arrival date** allows you enough time to prepare before the first race.

8 **Avoid long distance driving**. If this is impossible, ensure that you have a co-driver and only do one-hour stints each.

9 If you are **travelling by car**, make sure that it is reliable and fully serviced. Take plenty of spares with you in case of a breakdown.

10 **Check that your boat trailer and tailboard are in good condition** and that they meet all legal requirements (correct registration number, etc). Take with you a spare wheel and wheel bearings. Remember, no towing on the outside lane of the motorway – expensive fines!

11 It is essential to take a **good tool kit** with you to cover all necessary repairs to your equipment. Spare fittings, ropes, spars and sails must also be included.

12 If a **measurement certificate** is applicable, make sure that this is valid; also, any **insurance** for your boat and personal liability. Do not forget to take these documents with you.

13 Organise **good accommodation**.

14 You must get your **usual amount of sleep**.

15 **Watch your diet**, and try to eat the same amount of food as you normally do. **Liquid intake** is important, especially if you are in a climate that is much hotter than your normal one.

16 It is important to **establish a routine** immediately on arrival at the venue. Eat breakfast, go down to the boat park, go on the water, come off the water, warm down, debrief, eat dinner, and go to bed at around

the same time each day prior to the first race.

17 Whatever your age, there are sure to be certain **psychological pressures** in your life, and you must get these out of your mind before leaving home.

18 Decide whether or not you wish to have any **family involvement** at a major event.

19 Decide if you need a **coach** for the event; and, if so, make sure you take the coach of *your* choice.

20 If you want to, take your usual form of **relaxation** with you – reading or listening to music, etc.

21 Finally, enjoy the championship. After all, racing is the *best sport on earth*, and one of the most challenging!

It should be clear by now that very careful preparation is needed if you are to mount a successful campaign, and you have to go into a championship with the mental confidence that you are prepared in every respect if you are to stand any chance of winning. So let us look at the afore-mentioned points in greater detail.

Chartwork

Acquire a chart of the area and, as soon as possible, establish where the race area is going to be. Circle the area on the chart, and from this you can now look at:

- **Surrounding geographical land masses**, and how they will affect the race area from any wind direction.
- **Tidal data**, and how that will affect you while racing throughout the day as well as lay lines with the wind from any direction. Also, how the tide will affect the sea state with the wind in different directions.
- **Depth of water**, and how this will affect the strength and direction of the tide across the race area throughout the day. The sea state can also be influenced by

this; there may be calmer water on one side of the course due to the change in the depth of water – which may be to your advantage on the beat, but not on the run.

This type of preparation will give you greatly needed confidence, because you will have knowledge of the venue before you even arrive. Once there, you can then put this theoretical knowledge into practice and confirm your theory on the water.

Training programme

Normally, a minimum period of three months' practical work is necessary for you to be ready for the first race. However, in dinghy racing I have known a team to train all day every day for three weeks prior to a world championship and win. Whatever the details of your training programme, it must include the eleven aspects of the sport that were listed on p. x. Only on completion of this programme will you have prepared yourself mentally by getting into a confident frame of mind – one where you really believe that you *can* do well at the championship. However, do not be *too* confident, and do not *expect* to do well or win; if you are banking on winning, you are sure to lose!

Travel plans

Wherever your championship is to be held; it will invariably mean travelling (unless you are lucky enough for it to be held at your own club – once in a blue moon!).

If at all possible, ask a friend, colleague or member of the family to help with any necessary travel arrangements. This will take a great deal of pressure off you and enable you to concentrate on all your other preparations.

Try to arrive at least four days before the first race to allow for rest, orientation, measurement and race strategy checks. I find that if you arrive any earlier you start to get bored; any later, and you will find yourself rushing and in a panic. If long-distance flights are involved, then allow yourself seven days to recover from jet lag.

Passports and visas

You must ensure that all necessary documents are valid, and allow yourself plenty of time to obtain any renewals. Also, check whether or not you require an international driver's licence in any of the countries in which you may be driving. Similarly, it is important to check your health authority about any inoculations that may be necessary for any of the countries you may be visiting. If you do need to have injections, have them done in plenty of time to allow yourself to recover. You cannot compete effectively in a major championship while suffering from side effects of the inoculation.

Spare gear

It is extremely important that you take with you all the items that you may need to replace should you incur any damage while racing. Your spares should include: mast, boom, spinnaker pole (if applicable), mainsail, jib, spinnaker (if applicable), centreboard, rudder blade, tiller, tiller extension, fittings, sheets and halyards. Finally, do not forget some spare sailing gear – you will need to allow for a variety of weather conditions at the venue.

Measurement

Where applicable, you must ensure that you have a valid measurement certificate and present it during measurement time prior to the commencement of racing. It is your personal responsibility to ensure that your boat is legal at all times in accordance with your class rules. You do not want to be in the position where, during measurement,

you discover your boat is illegal and you cannot compete. The most common faults with regard to measurement are:

- Boat underweight
- Centreboard overweight
- Centreboard or rudder do not meet the required measurements
- Sail numbers in the wrong place
- Sailmaker's emblem in the wrong place or too prominent
- Black bands on the spars missing or in the wrong place

Make sure that all these common faults are checked and corrected before leaving home. It will save you a lot of hassle and problems at the event – problems that you do not need at this time.

Accommodation

Your accommodation must be good if you want to do well, so do not try to economise by camping, or sleeping in the car or on the beach. It may be acceptable during the training period, but certainly not at the event you want to do well in. You must also consider your hours of sleep during a championship; these should be kept as close to your normal amount as possible. You cannot expect to party all night and then win races, having only had a few hours' sleep.

Food

During your training programme you will need to address the question of your optimum bodyweight and diet. (This subject is looked at in more detail in Chapter 2.) However, during the week before the event you will need to start your carbohydrate loading programme prior to the first race. This build-up of carbohydrates will give you the energy required to sustain a five- to seven-day championship, especially in the mid to upper wind ranges. If necessary,

Here helm and crew have good boat balance and trim, enabling the boat to pitch over the waves whilst beating to windward. Maximum teamwork and concentration on working the boat through the chop is essential to maintain maximum boat speed.

consult your coach or doctor for advice on this very important physical preparation. While at the event, *if possible* try to eat only food that you are familiar with. Strange foods may disagree with you, perhaps even cause an allergy of which you are unaware, which could put you in bed for the remainder of the championship.

Drink

Energy drinks are useful as a source of glucose when you are carrying out strenuous activities. If you are in a foreign country, it is advisable to drink bottled water only, as tap water can contain bacteria that may make you ill – as many competitors in the past have discovered. Make sure that you have

plenty to drink while afloat, especially on a back-to-back race day. Where racing is taking place in warmer climates you will need to increase your liquid intake in order to prevent dehydration.

Outside communication and pressure

Whether it be your work, education or domestic situation, when you go to a major championship you should not allow any of these things to affect your ability to be totally focused on your objective – *winning*. You are there to win the event and should therefore try to sort out any problems you may have before you get there.

Before you leave for the event, tell members of your family remaining at home that, unless it is absolutely necessary for you to return home immediately, you do not wish to receive any bad news while you are attending the championship. There is obviously nothing you can do to help a bad situation at home if you are halfway around

Good boat balance and trim in this National 12. Bodyweight is well aft to lift the deep 'V' shaped bow off the water to enable the helmsman to bear away in the gusts and prevent stalling out the rudder blade, broaching and capsizing.

the world, so it is better not to know about it until you return home. Such news could affect your concentration and deny you a medal position.

Family/coach involvement

During the planning stages of any campaign, it is very important to establish who you want to be involved and who you want to accompany you on your travels. Some competitors like to have their family and/or friends around them at major events; others are better on their own. *You* must make the decision and then make it clear to parents etc whether you do or do not wish them to accompany you. If necessary, ask your coach or a colleague to speak to them. I myself have had to ask many a parent not to accompany their son or daughter to a youth championship.

Decide at the start whether you require a coach; and if you do want one, decide who it will be. The coach can assist you right through your training programme up to the championship itself – not only through coaching, but also by taking a great deal of the pressures of organisation off you (and by helping you to drink the champagne at the end of course!) However, you may not want to have a coach/manager with you for your campaign, and may feel more comfortable without one. There are numerous top sailors who do not require this support, especially the older, more experienced, campaigners.

These are some of the most important pre-championship preparations to be included in the planning stages of your campaign, whether it is for a national, European or world championship or for the Olympic Games.

Remember, preparing for a championship, like any other major event in your life, requires detailed planning, organisation and dedication if you want to do well.

PREPARE TO WIN!

2

Self Preparation

Performance dinghies came on the scene some forty years ago and were followed by performance yachts. In order to gain the maximum potential from these crafts when racing, it became necessary for sailors to increase their physical and mental ability. This concept gave rise to the famous quote '**Only the fittest will win**' (Paul Elvström and Rodney Pattison).

It was important, therefore, that when the Youth Race Training Scheme was established in 1977, self preparation appeared at the top of the list of race training priorities. The Youth Race Training Scheme has now been in existence for 17 years and during that time we have produced 26 World Champions and 16 European Champions. In 1994 alone, 11 gold medals, 3 silver medals and 1 bronze medal were won at international level by past and present Youth Squad members.

So how fit do you need to be to do well at the highest level of competition? **Answer**: Fit enough to sail as hard up the last beat of the last race as you did up the first beat of the first race in the upper wind range *and* survive the social programme!!

With the style of championship racing changing to two or three races a day (maybe more!), so must our ideas on training. The emphasis now must be placed more on mobility and flexibility as well as stamina, especially with today's smaller courses, shorter legs, more mark roundings and finally more races – perhaps 12 in the championship.

As most of us already know, it takes a minimum of three months to reach an acceptable level of fitness for a championship, but to become unfit can take as little as three seconds.

Unfortunately, many athletes representing the UK at International level do not take proper care of themselves, especially the younger ones. Picking up an injury prior to, or during an event is 'fatal', a complete waste of all the training, money and effort that you have put into the event. So look after yourself. It is obviously important to keep fit during an event but very unwise to take part in any strenuous activity that may result in some kind of injury. Any person selected to represent the UK at International level should avoid *all* physical contact sports during their preparations, as it is very easy to pick up an injury whilst playing such a sport.

Your fitness training programme must be developed to suit the job that you do in the boat. The fitness training programme for a Europe sailor, for example, will be totally different from that recommended for a mainsail trimmer on a fifty footer being used for match racing.

Flexibility, mobility, strength and stamina are the overall criteria in both yacht and dinghy racing. Identify your requirements and work on them specifically. Establish your personal training programme. Ask your PE Teacher, coach or local gym instructor for specific guidelines, if required.

Key things to remember are: **Never go into your training programme cold – warm up and stretch out first**. On completion of the session, **warm down – ease out of it; do**

not just stop and sit or lie down. If your muscles tend to be tight, re-warm and re-stretch them at the end of your training session.

Stretching and warm up

Over the years, the value of stretching as sports injury prevention and aid to increased performance has become increasingly recognised.

In the past, stretching was balistic; meaning that limbs were in motion in ever-increasing arcs; the aim was to try to reach further each time. Eventually it was recognised that this could be a recipe for injury, since limbs are heavy and hard to stop without a jerk. Now, slow careful stretch exercises are recommended. You should never start an exercise programme without a thorough warm up. In a track suit this may take time, but in sailing gear, which is designed for heat retention, it does not take so long. Once warm, you can adopt one of the several positions illustrated, holding the posture so that the muscle to be stretched feels uncomfortably tight but *not* painful in any way. Hold this position for a total of thirty seconds broken into three bouts of ten-second holds with a two second gap between each. During the two-second breaks you should relax to rest the muscles.

You may notice that during the second ten seconds, you can stretch further than during the first bout. The third stretch may also achieve further stretch. However, during the total thirty seconds, do not push yourself too far and go from uncomfortably stretched to painful, to very painful. The sensation should be from uncomfortably stretched, to uncomfortably stretched, to uncomfortably stretched. Stretch your hamstrings as well as the quads. You will use them – low back pain is frequently associated with tight hamstrings which affect the tilt of the pelvis to which the lower back is attached.

Prior to sailing

To warm up the body, to encourage the heart to a greater output in order to supply and warm the muscles that are going to do the work, it is essential to have a preliminary warm-up routine. This should take place before going on the water and be repeated on the water. A stretch routine during warm-up is mandatory. It used to be said that the effort of launching a Finn over a shingle beach causes greater heart rate than sailing it! After changing into sailing clothing (which should be adjusted to give full and free movement in every plane) the warm-up should commence. A warm-up routine is required even in warm weather. Professional athletes in track and field would not dream of competing without a prolonged warm-up even on a hot day. It follows that the core temperature of the body will rise unduly if protective clothing is very efficient and each day therefore the duration of warm-up, and the composition of your clothing will require thought.

After warm-up the muscles are now prepared and ready for stretching exercises. These should be done before launching the dinghy, and they are designed to put the joints through a full range of movement so that the limbs are prepared for any undue stress at the extreme range of motion, without trauma to the joint or over-stretched muscle.

Strengthening exercises consist of several types of muscle toning or building exercises. The individual sailor has to decide whether an overall increase in muscle bulk is required or, if there is already a problem with body weight, whether some fat can usefully be exchanged for muscle.

Fitness training

All serious competitors appreciate that to achieve good results some kind of fitness training is essential. How much training you do obviously depends on your time available

Fitness Test

Name	Sit-ups max 2 mins	Squat thrusts max 1 min	Burpees max 1 min	Press-ups max	Distance run /swum 12 mins
Sarah	103	96	37	70	21 laps run
Sally	112	89	24	62	18 lengths swum
Ben	108	136	37	50	27 lengths swum
Iain	100	158	47	55	23.5 laps run
Paul	73	93	33	34	21.75 laps run
Penny	95	122	36	56	37.75 lengths swum
Richard	105	80	34	55	27 lengths swum

and motivation but it can tie in with other favoured sports. Three sessions a week of, cycling, jogging or swimming (20-30 minutes hard work) will improve your overall stamina and endurance. Some sailors do each of these activities once a week if they do not have a problem with their bodyweight. Keep a regular check on your weight as your programme progresses as, for some sailors (dinghy and small keel boats), this will be a fairly critical factor. *Do not train if you are feeling unwell or have a sore throat or high temperature.*

Midway through your programme, take a fitness test and another one towards the end to compare your improvement and target figures in relation to past squads and teams. Above are some fitness test results of past squads and teams:

Exhausting fitness training must stop seven days before Race 1 of the championship but continue with a light daily fitness routine in readiness for the event.

Training to win

Physical fitness increases mental fitness; mental fitness increases confidence, and confidence means confidence to **win**. You do not need to be super-fit to be a world champion; being the fittest person on the water does not mean that you are going to win races (do not forget that there are nine other aspects to the sport). I was given the following quotation which I think sums it up perfectly: 'If you don't have the necessary racing skills, physical fitness alone won't make you win races – it just means you will be able to sail badly more comfortably for longer.'

I have known some yachting athletes to be so fit that they cannot sit still in the boat in light weather races because their muscles start twitching, and each time they move they disturb the rig. 'As a rule the best training is achieved simply by carrying out the activity for which one is training' (P O Astrand). In other words, runners must run, swimmers must swim, and dinghy sailors must sail dinghies etc. Can the dinghy sailor who wants to compete at the top level get both the amount and intensity of physical training necessary for success at that level just by sailing? In theory the answer is yes, but not if economy of time, effort and expense are important factors in his budget. Before trying to justify that answer we need to appreciate that 'fitness' is not an absolute term, it can only be described relative to a specified activity. We also need to have at least a basic understanding of two principles of training: those of 'overload' and 'specificity'.

Why is fitness relative? Suppose we are asked: are you fit enough to jog a mile? Most of us would probably answer, yes. However, if we were asked: 'Are you fit enough to compete in a 100 metre race

'Only the fittest will win'. This Soling crew give maximum physical effort to power the boat through the chop.

against Linford Christie or a 100 metre hurdles race against Colin Jackson?' Few of us would hesitate to answer 'no'. Here our fitness is being assessed relative to the activity of running and relative to the standards of top-class runners in two different events. Our interest is in fitness, not relative to running but to the demands of racing a single- or double-handed dinghy.

Overload

What do we mean by 'overload'? Our bodies adapt, over time, to the type and intensity of load to which we subject them. If you take on a new activity, or the same activity at an increased intensity, then at first your body will be overloaded. It will not be able to cope without suffering some pain. However, if you persist in that new activity, in time you will be able to manage it with less and less stress. The body is adapting to the new

demand which at first was an overload but with repetition becomes normal. So it is with training.

To be effective, the training exercise, must overload the particular body system you want to train. If you continue with the same intensity and duration of exercise, the body will adapt to it. To maintain that level you will need to keep up with the exercise. If you stop or cut back significantly on the exercise the body will re-adapt to the lower level. If you want to further increase your capability you will have to increase the intensity and/or duration. Therefore, to train a 'system' you must 'overload' it sufficiently to promote adaptation but not so much that there is a breakdown of that system. By 'system' I mean a functional unit of the body, which may comprise a certain muscle group used for example, to move an arm or a leg in a particular way or to maintain a balanced posture; it includes the nerve pathways controlling that muscle group and the bones and structures affected when the muscle group contracts.

Specificity

The adaptation resulting from an overload will be specific to the system overloaded. If you want strong fingers you will not get them from exercising your toes. But even that does not tell the whole story. The adaptation is specific not only to the system or muscle group involved but also to the way in which it is overloaded. The more precisely your training can replicate the sporting activity for which you are training, the bigger the gain in 'fitness' for that activity and the better the economy of training effort. If you want to train your arms for strength and endurance so that you can single sheet the main for the whole of both reaches in a force 5, it is an inefficient training effort to exercise with a sheet at an angle of say 45 degrees to the horizontal if, when racing, you will be working at 10 degrees. So 'specificity' in this context means that training must be specific to the system and to the activity for which you want to train.

Let us return to the qualified 'yes' in response to the question as to whether fitness can be achieved solely through sailing. Why do sailors find it almost impossible to get all the physical training they need for elite competition just by sailing? Suppose you are training for a world championship scheduled for August. So starting in January, you diligently spend every hour you can on the water. But the weather pattern that year is predominantly light winds with just the occasional force 3 to 4. When you get to the championship, perhaps in a different continent, the weather pattern is completely different with winds never less than force 4 for the whole competition. Will your body be adapted through your winter, spring and summer sailing, and no other training, to the demands of those conditions? You may be the world's best in racing tactics and boat handling in winds less than force 3, but if you haven't got a body specifically trained and adapted to the endurance and strength

demands of hiking to windward and planing downwind in force 5, you will be hanging on just to survive as those 'fit for force 5' lap you on the second beat. The sailor therefore has a problem with 'training by doing' that others do not face.

In many sports, the athlete can train more intensively by setting himself targets of faster times. The sailor can only train harder by waiting for stronger winds, or travelling to areas where strong winds are common. For those who cannot afford to chase the winds, physical training is necessary for consistent good results in top competition, but it must be specific, it must be regular and it must be built up gradually to an intensity which represents an overload replicating the effects of the strongest winds in which you may race.

Specificity in training means two things:

- You must train the *specific* muscles you will use.
- These muscles must be trained *specifically* for the kind of activity they are going to perform.

A fitness programme consisting of jogging, squat-jumps and press-ups will do almost nothing for your ability to sit out and to pull on ropes, because it has not trained your stomach muscles at all. It has trained your thigh muscles to move but not to hold still, and it has trained the arm muscles involved in pushing but not those involved in pulling. This is not to say that such a programme is no use to anybody. For someone wanting to be a better jogger it is perfect. As a large part of the fitness training for a rugby forward it is very good. But for a dinghy racer it has the wrong specificity. This type of exercise can, however, figure in the programme, but it must not be the major feature.

The physiology of sailing

The physiology of sailing, or how the body works when we sail, has been a closed book until recent years.

In 1980 Prof Marchetti and colleagues in Rome compared the response of the heart to the stress of two sailing positions: hiking and trapezing. They found that the heart was beating much faster for the hiker than for the wire man, and that the blood pressure was also higher. By using sensors on the muscles, they discovered that the muscles on the front of the body of the hiker were working hard whilst those of the trapezer were only active in supporting the neck and in keeping both the calf/ankle stable.

The high pulse rates in hiking are required because the muscles are contracting isometrically. That is they are tightening up hard to hold the body in the required position and are neither shortening or lengthening as they do so. When a muscle tightens hard in this way it becomes so tight that it squashes the blood vessels and prevents the circulation from functioning properly. The muscle becomes starved of oxygen (ischaemia) and as a result, the contracting muscle begins to hurt. Having no proper blood supply the working muscle can no longer obtain energy by the usual 'aerobic' method and has to work without oxygen, or anaerobically. As a result lactic acid begins to accumulate rapidly.

When the quads in the front of the thigh and the abdominal muscles become too painful, we have to sit inboard on the side tanks of the dinghy to rest. Whilst the circulation is restored.

In contrast, during conventional endurance running sports, the high heart rate is associated with high oxygen consumption as the muscles work hard aerobically to sustain performance. They are of course contracting and relaxing and so allow a good blood circulation.

The more oxygen available within the body, the better the performance. Indeed as the measure of potential maximum performance in endurance sports the Max VO$_2$ (which is a measure of the maximum oxygen uptake that the body can manage to reach) became the key test. Also oxygen uptake is closely related to the heart rate in a linear fashion, so that it is possible in testing fitness to predict the Max VO$_2$ from the theoretical maximum heart rate.

Our theoretical maximum heart rate is obtained by subtracting our age in years from 220. Thus a 40 year old man would have a likely maximum heart rate of 220−40=180. A man of 60, a maximum of 160. We perform less well in sport as we get older because we can no longer hit high rates, and so we carry less oxygen to our muscles where they use it to burn the fuel with which the muscle works.

Recently two dinghy sailing physiologists, Voglatzis and Spurway, working in Glasgow measured dinghy sailors on the water with expensive portable gas analysis equipment. They have shown that hiking dinghy sailors may have high pulse rates, but *unlike* the endurance runners these high rates are *not* associated with high oxygen consumption.

This important finding turns on its head some of the previous ideas about the best way to train for dinghy sailing. We used to say that since the heart rates were high in dinghy sailing as in running we should train our hearts in the same way. Therefore, general aerobic type fitness training was advised with the addition of specific exercises for local body strength. Does this approach still apply?

The answer is that for the very average unfit or inactive adult there is much to be gained from a fitness programme of the old type, partly because not all of sailing is in the form of crunching beats. There is some 'down hill' work, and there are many times when the quads and abs are not contracting isometrically. Every time the sailor adjusts his position he either shortens or elongates his muscles. The particular muscle ceases to act isometrically, and at once some fresh blood enters the muscle so that it can resume aerobic metabolism again. The pain goes until the next episode of sustained isometric contraction.

But for the high flyer, training takes on an added dimension, for there is now another way to train. In an isometrically contracting muscle, the circulation of blood is obstructed less when it is not contracting as hard as it is when it is maximally contracted. The aim now is to try to develop the muscle so that it is strong enough to hold the hiking position when working at less than 100% maximal contraction. If we can improve the muscle so that the body position is maintained at say 40% of the maximal contraction we get the best of both worlds. We have a muscle working hard enough isometrically to hold our hiking position, but with an oxygen supply that is adequate for its needs, so we do not have to come inboard to rest from pain.

The best way to improve this training requirement is by the use of the hiking bench – longer and longer spells on the bench, which should replicate the shape of the dinghy for which we are training (training is very specific as far as joint angles and stresses are concerned). Discomfort in the anterior abdominal muscles will be noticed first, but as these improve the discomfort may be more in the thigh. **Warning:** Those who have unduly high blood pressure should avoid prolonged use of the hiking bench, since this is associated with a raising of the blood pressure.

For the very top sailors, there is maybe less use for the hiking bench since many of the semi-pros or professionals are in their boats all the time these days. The dinghy itself is, after all, the ultimate in hikingbench design. But if you don't want to go for a run on a filthy night how about an hour in front of the fire reading or watching the telly whilst sitting on your section of 505? Or why don't you offer to trapeze next season and ask your crew to drive the thing for a change?

In the sailing physiology world there is an academic north/south divide. On the one hand there may be too much emphasis upon aerobic endurance type preparation. On the other hand maybe the hiking bench is over emphasised. It could be that as an individual you try what mix is best for you. The canny northerners advise a training programme based upon isometric static lower body training on the hiking bench, coupled with dynamic upper body training of the arms and shoulders, since these are in constant motion whilst sailing in a breeze.

Planning a fitness programme

The first thing that a sailor (or any other sportsman) must think about when planning a fitness programme, is his individual needs. These are very unlikely to be met by copying the training adopted (quite properly) for team games at school. Think first about the special requirements of the job you do on the boat. Here are some pointers.

- Are you a dinghy helm or a crew in a non-trapeze dinghy? If so, your emphasis must be on hiking endurance and on armwork.
- Are you a trapeze crew? Then speed and agility (arm and leg) will be at a premium, and abdominal muscle endurance will matter much less.
- Are you a winch-man? If so, all your specific concentration must be on arm-power.

However much you want to improve your fitness for your particular role you must also ask yourself another set of questions: what are your personal strengths and weaknesses? Some are obvious: if you are a 90 kg trapezer you almost certainly have strength to spare, but should work on agility and try to lose some weight at the same time. The converse applies if you are 65 kg and want to campaign a Finn. To be a bit more specific, do you sit out your 470 fairly well, but lack the arm strength to hoist that kite fast when it is blowing a hoolie? Do you hang pretty

Well poised; ready to pump the main on this wave and gain a few metres over those who don't bother or who are physically too tired.

far out from your Laser, even on the final beat, but come in more slowly than you should in quick tacks and unexpected lulls?

Questions like these are hard to answer honestly, because they mean you are going to have to work most at the things you are worst at – whereas it is far more comfortable to go on training at (and possibly even boasting about) those parts of your role which come more easily. So check your self-assessment with your sailing coach, your crew or another racer who knows you well. They may know nothing about fitness training, yet they will be able to spot your deficiencies better than you can.

Include some generality

This section began by emphasising the need for specific training because 90 per cent of people who try to train without professional advice adopt a programme which is insufficiently specific. On the other hand, the professional adviser would always include some non-specific (ie general) training in a programme. There are two reasons:

- If you strengthen only the muscles required for your principal actions you will become unbalanced. This does not just look unsightly; it can cause injury. For in sudden movement the strong muscles may tear the weak ones, or strain the structure which is receiving an unbalanced pull.
- There are two systems of the body upon which every sort of exercise puts demands, and which must be conditioned first before embarking upon a strenuous specificity-emphasising regime. These are the heart (plus the rest of the circulatory system) and the lungs (plus other components of the respiratory system).

A well-designed training programme, if you are starting from scratch (following perhaps either an after-season lay-off, or a season which had involved too much long distance

travel) might at first have you devoting 80 or even 100 percent of effort to the recovery of general fitness. Even in the last intensive period before your major event of the year you should put 20 to 30 per cent of effort in this direction. Hence it is valid to say that the jog/jump/press-up programme which contributes to general, though not specific, fitness would only modestly help your hiking endurance – rather than do no good at all!

Build generality into endurance, into strength, into speed

Work out how long a training period you have before the competition starts in earnest. Let us assume it is somewhere between 12 and 24 weeks. Divide this into four roughly equal periods, of approximately three to six weeks each. Then assuming you are a healthy, young (or youngish!) adult, develop your programme thus:

1 *In the first phase build general fitness*
The jog/jump/press-up kind of routine would be all right here, though proper circuit-training two or three times a week would be better. Other sports such as cycling or swimming are very worthwhile, and have particular advantages if you are one of those whose knees or ankles do not take kindly to road-running. Racquet games also introduce variety with negligible risk of injury. But remember that if you are over 30 you *get fit to play squash* rather than *play squash to get fit. Over 40 this is even more important.* During this period, light work at your specific needs will be useful. However it is quite acceptable to leave this out if you prefer something new at this stage, in order to reduce the psychological problem of boredom later on.

2 *In the second phase build specific endurance*
Specific exercises must begin at the start of this period if they have not done so before. These are the exercises which match your

particular sailing role, such as abdominal exercises for hiking – exact suggestions are made later. Do not give up the general fitness training, but gradually increase the time spent on specifics, paring down on the general exercise to make room. However, in this period neither forces nor speeds greater than you can easily manage should be attempted. The aim by the end of this second phase of about six weeks is merely to be able to do the exercises easily for quite long periods.

Up to this point the training programme is safe for sailors of any age. Girls under 15, boys under 16, and adults over 40-45 years old who have not kept up hard physical activity during their mature lives should extend phase (2) indefinitely and not go on to phases (3) and (4).

3 *In the third phase adults and young sailors who have stopped growing may build specific strength*
Begin now to increase the loads in your specific strength exercises – initially perhaps twice a week, and then later in every session. If you are hiking, or lifting bodyweight, add to it with a weight jacket or a part-filled rucksack. Some general training should still be done in this phase, but on all but one or two days per week it should now be confined to the warm-up and round-off periods with specific strength exercises as the core of the training session.

4 *In the fourth phase add specific speed*
In this final period, some of each of the previous activities are still undertaken but speedwork is added, first to two specific training sessions, then to all of them. For speedwork reduce the load (eg go back to unaugmented bodyweight) and strive to increase your speed. Do repetition sit-ups, rope pulls (or whatever) against the clock, and set yourself targets for small but definite improvements each week. This new feature must be placed near the start of each training session, for fatigue makes speed-

improvement impossible. Later in each workout you will be adding yet further to endurance, but not speed.

Finally, take at least three days of rest before each major series. Light general training can be done in this period, but not the hard stuff. You will have gained nothing if you go into a big event with those specific muscle groups fatigued. Training (normally of phase 4 type) should be resumed between major series, but always with three to four days' lay-off before the next big event starts.

All increases of effort must be gradual

First increase the frequency of training. Start the general fitness programme with three to four sessions a week, then increase to five then to six. But even in the final strength and speed phases, do not exceed that. A day or two off per week is necessary, to allow time for recovery from minor strains and sheer fatigue. Remember that the adaptation to the stimulus of training takes place between training sessions not during training – there must be time for adaptation otherwise there is no point in training!

Next, increase duration. Increase the lengths of runs, and the number of repetitions of strength exercises, as fitness builds, but cut back on duration for the first three to four times after every increase of load or speed.

In phase 4, speed increases must be gradual. If you are really trying in the first place, improvements by more than a few per cent will be unusual.

Quoting actual figures for any of these aspects, except those of safety, is a doubtful practice. Individual capabilities differ so much that you are probably better to assess yourself and set your own goals. But the sort of goals that might be reasonable would be to:

- Increase the duration of runs from 20 to 30 minutes during the general-fitness stage

- Increase the repetitions of unloaded sit-ups from 20 at the start of the second stage to 50 at the end of the third
- Increase the maximum weight that can be lifted via a pulley from 30 to 37 kg in 12 weeks.

Remember always that much smaller increases should be expected in strength and speed than in endurance.

Never attempt exercise without a warm-up

To do so is to court injury. A three-minute jog and a further three to four minutes of exercises from the general fitness programme, used as preparation for the strenuous workout, will get the heart and lungs going and the blood flowing fast through the muscles and connective tissues. They will also quite literally, raise the temperature within the muscles. All these factors are highly desirable before the stressful training start. In the warm-up be sure to include light, loose activity for the muscles you are going to impose real loads on later, eg two sets of six or so non-pressurised sit-ups should be part of the sequence before you go on to a hiking bench. Also include some stretching exercises for the neck shoulders, back, hamstrings and quads between the warm-up and the hard work of the day – but remember to stretch slowly and not to 'bounce'. Take a tip – warm up and stretch in the same way before each race as well.

Specific sailing exercises

Only suggestions can be given here – take them as illustrations of principles rather than as prescriptions from which you must not depart. It is assumed throughout that you are training at home: a well-equipped gym provides more scope for many types of training, though not necessarily for all. For general fitness for sailing, sit-ups, press-ups, pull-ups, burpees, star jumps, squat thrusts and side bends are all worthwhile exercises.

Training for sitting out

The abdominal (stomach) muscles, the quadriceps (upper thighs) and the ilio-psoas (a muscle rising in the pelvis and lower back and passing to the thigh bone) take the main strain here. Much of it is static (technically 'isometric') strain, but you must also be able to move in again quickly – and your arms must be able to pull hard on ropes while you are out there.

A hiking bench is best. But make sure it matches your boat really closely. It is pointless during training, to be supported at mid-thigh if in reality the gunwhale of your boat supports you behind the knees. Also make sure that the bench is either well rounded or well padded, or both: you can do lasting damage if you cut off the circulation at the backs of your legs during every training session. Nevertheless, with these provisos in mind, it is possible to construct very good makeshift benches from suitably positioned furniture – like dining chairs laid on their backs with 'toestraps' round their feet, or the arms of sofas brought near to heavy tables. When the boat simulation is right, get so used to the bench that you can read a book in your standard 'force 5 position'. Build up from just five or so little hikes lasting only one to two minutes each to three or four hikes lasting ten minutes each. Do ten repetitions, once or twice in each hike, of coming in sharply and at once going out again. Also try rotating yourself to right and left while you are out there, as you would do many times on a real boat.

Throughout all this, remember that there is a vital rule when hiking a dinghy. In extending your upper body over the water to obtain greater leverage, when going to windward or when reaching, the body should pivot outboard from the hips. Undue forward curvature of the lumbar spine, caused by hollowing the lower back, causes undue sheering stress upon some lumbar discs and compression of others. In such a position, rotation or sideways tilting of the spine when helming or pulling sheets may prove the last straw to a suspect, ageing or immature spine. The penalty is likely to be pain in your lower back for the rest of your life because the wrong muscles have been loaded and the bottom vertebrae compressed. The best posture is to keep your legs bent. However, shallow hulls, like those of Lasers, impose straight legs: but **keep your back curled, whatever your boat**.

If you do not have a bench for exercising, do bent-leg sit-ups with your feet flat on the floor and your hands on your ears. Do them in the 'trunk-curl' fashion, lifting your head off the floor first, then your shoulders, then your back – avoid a hollow back, for the same reason as in hiking. Do 10 such movements then stay with your back just clear of the floor for 10 to 20 seconds, then do the trunk-curls again. If your feet are flat on the floor you are exercising your anterior abdominal muscles. If you repeat the exercise with your feet under a restraining bar you are also exercising the ilio-psoas, the powerful hiking muscles of the pelvis. Take a short rest and repeat the set. Do, say, two sets of 20 curls each, building up to four sets of 40 or 50 by the end. In addition, train your quadriceps on a leg extension bench – the kind where you straighten your leg against a weight. Or do the one-legged squat thrusts – just 5 with each leg at first, building up to 3 or 4 sets of 8 to 10 thrusts each.

Finally there is a quadriceps exercise which you can do as you stand in a queue. With your legs absolutely straight, brace hard, one leg at a time making the thigh muscles stand out just above the knee; hold for 5 seconds then relax. Brace alternate legs, say, 6–8 times each, 15–20 times a day. People may look a little curiously at your expression, but you will be considerably less likely to suffer knee pain after strong-wind races the following summer.

Major abdominal strengthening is an instance where counter-balancing development (of the back) requires specific exercise also. Do this by the prone lift: lie on your stomach, and slowly raise either the feet or the torso off the floor. Hold for 5 seconds, lower and repeat 5 to 10 times. Do not lift both ends at once into a 'banana' position.

Training for sheeting in

Pull-ups on wall-bars, doors or wardrobes are useful; they strengthen the pulling muscles of the upper arms and chest. However, they will not enhance your grip on a rope. Much better, therefore, is to do your pull-ups on a tail of rope. Most people can find a tree, bannister or garage rafter from which to hang one. However, even here the angle of pull is unrealistic.

Lifting weights on ropes represents the effort better. If you can arrange a pulley so that the rope leads up to your waist at a 30–45° angle, this exercise will be pretty specific, even to the correct lead angle. By doing both this and the pull-ups you will be a great deal stronger in 12–18 weeks.

Having got that far with your equipment, though, maybe you can position the pulley to enable you to add simultaneous arm exercise to your periods on the hiking bench. Then you really will be in business! Two alternative positions are necessary: one for left arm (port tack) training and one for right arm (starboard tack) training. Since these positions will be at floor level you need a second block higher up if you are going to lift a weight. So it may be easier to work against a spring or bungee cord on the hiking bench/frame. On the other hand, weights are more easily adjustable as you get stronger, eg bricks in a bucket.

Whichever kind of load you choose, *strong fastenings* of mechanical parts to the frame are essential. Incidentally, if hand tiredness is a limitation to your performance in hard weather, try putting a rubber ball in

Stretching Exercises

Golden rules

1 Stretch is an important part of 'warm up' and 'warm down'. Warm up *before* stretching.
2 Never stretch cold muscles. Do a five minute gentle jog in track suit or warm clothing.
3 Never bounce when stretching – this may cause injury.
4 Never hold your breath whilst stretching.
5 Hold the stretched position so that you can feel the stretch but not be in pain.

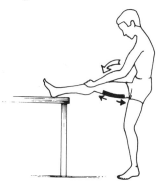 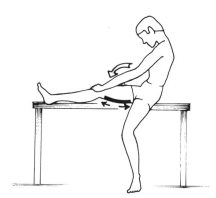

Stretching the back of the thigh (hamstrings)

You may do this either standing with the leg placed on a table or desk top; or by sitting on a bench, desk or table top with the leg to be stretched lifted up on to the raised surface.

Keep your leg to be stretched straight at the knee and lean forward until you feel the muscle at the back of your thigh stretch. Do not try to touch your toes or to put your head on your knees because this exercise is not to stretch your back. Try instead to think of putting your 'belly' on to the top of your thigh.

Hold the position of stretch for ten seconds. Then relax for two seconds before you hold the stretch again for a further ten seconds. Relax two seconds and hold for a final ten seconds. You will probably notice that you go further after each ten seconds stretch. You are not to go from stretched to painful to very painful. A feeling of stretch is all you require.

Stretching the front of the thigh (quadriceps)

Whilst standing up, bend the leg to be stretched up behind you and grasp the ankle with the hand of the same side of the body. Pull with the hand until you feel the stretch in the front of the thigh. You can do this wrongly if you do not ensure that your thigh is directly in line with your body. This is because one of the four 'quads' muscles arises from the pelvis and is thus less stretched if the hip is bent. If you bend the hip you stretch only three of the four 'Quads' muscles. Hold the stretched position for thirty seconds, broken into ten second segments as for the 'hams'.

Stretching the calf muscle at the back of the lower leg

Face the wall with the leg to be stretched well behind you. Keep the heel on the floor and the foot pointing directly at the wall. With the knee straight lean towards the wall controlling your position with your hands on the wall at shoulder height with elbows bent. The other leg is placed closer to the wall with the knee bent to help to control the position. As you lean towards the wall you will feel your calf muscles stretching. Hold the position for thirty seconds as above. Then, maintaining the position bend the rear knee, sink towards the floor until you again feel a stretch deeper in the calf.

Improving the stomach or abdominal muscles (abs)

Lie on your back on the floor with bent knees. Make sure your pelvis is tilted so that your lower back is pushed into the floor. Feel with your hand to see that you are doing this properly. Hollow your abdomen by trying to pull your navel inwards. You may have to practice your pelvic tilting and abdominal hollowing separately before you are able to do the exercise properly since these two positions are an integral part of the exercise. Now place your hands upon your ears (not behind the neck) and slowly lift head and shoulders with your chin tucked in to look between your knees. There is no need to come up to a sitting position. Hold the position for a slow count of five, breathing normally as you do so.

Stretching the Ilio-psoas muscle (a powerful hiking muscle)

Adopt the position shown in the diagram with one leg placed well in front with the knee bent and the other almost as far behind as it will go (feet facing forward). You may either balance in this position or place the hands upon the floor. Move the pelvis forwards and down towards the ground and you will feel a stretch in front of the upper thigh and groin of the backward leg. Do not bounce. Hold the stretch for thirty seconds as above.

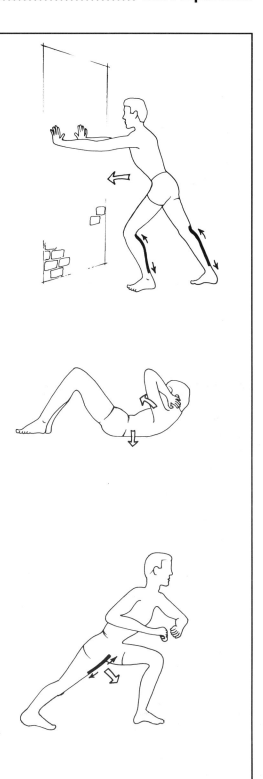

each pocket and kneading it as you go about your daily business. A few months of this can make a surprising difference – and does not even count as 'training time' at all.

Training for trapeze work

Many trapezers suffer not only fatigue during races but back pain off the water. Unfortunately the exact problem seems to vary with the individual and his particular harness. The best general advice is that a good deal of trunk exercise is worthwhile – but in this case treat abdomen and back equally. Trunk twists, side-bends and toe-touching are all *specific* exercises for the trapeze sailor but, just as when they are used in association with a warm-up, do them *slowly*, don't try to get further by momentum. 'Ballistic stretching', as this is called, is much more likely to cause injury. If twisting and tilting the spine is uncomfortable, *do not do it*!

Do a good number of prone lifts, aiming to cope with three sets of ten by the end of three or four months. Include some trunk-curls but only a quarter as many as if you were hike-training. Regard press-ups here as a specific exercise, not for the arms but for the trunk – keep your body straight, or your rear end very slightly high; don't let your body sag. Wall-bar exercises are useful trunk strengtheners too, if you can find a rafter or branch to do them from. In particular the hanging leg-raise; as you hang from a bar, raise your thighs (with bent knees) until they are horizontal in front of you, hold for three seconds and then lower; then repeat five times. As you get stronger, gradually extend your lower legs until they are straight out too – it is much harder! If you have ever found your legs getting tired in a long hard-weather race, then leg-thrusts will help; squat jumps and/or burpees should make a real contribution to your training. Sheeting-in exercises are also wholly appropriate to the trapezer.

Training for the winch-man

Few winch-men are total specialists, so general circuit training and the rope-pull exercises suggested above should figure substantially in the programme. Leg raises and pull-ups on bars (which are much more like winch handles than ropes) plus press-ups and some punch-bag training are also appropriate. Better still is 'sawing' with a partner of comparable strength, if available. However, none of these exercises will train your arms specifically for rotational movements, so see if you can find an old hand-cranked grindstone and arrange to rotate it against the braking influence of, say, a wedge of wood. Or rig a bike so that you work the pedals by hand against the brakes, or against an adjustable-tension resistance belt bearing upon the rim. If your winch is a vertical 'coffee grinder'; then try to set up your simulators to match; if it is the more usual horizontal action, try to mount the bike or grindstone on its side.

Weight training

Weight training is a potential hazard – a 180 lb athlete lifting 200 lb overhead in an incorrect way can exert a force of 2000 lb across the lumbar spine. Yet someone who does no heavy work can suffer from chronic backache because of long periods of standing at work, perhaps exacerbated by unequal leg length causing a lateral tilt of the spine.

The following points about avoiding back injury during weight training should be considered:

1 Weight training by children is not appropriate and caution should be used for growing youths. This is because certain back conditions can be made considerably worse by such training. In youth sailing, careful thought should be given to the likely eventual build of the young sailor by a study of his mother, father, brothers and sisters.

2 Weight training may entail the use of a Multigym where a sailor may train alone, or by using his own body weight in training movements. Training with free weights requires caution and training partners. Such weight training should be undertaken in groups of three, if heavy free weights on a bar are being used. This is because of the risk of losing control of the weight, with the consequent leverage causing significant injury to back or shoulder. One person should stand either side of the lifter to take immediate charge in the event of a failed lift. The use of a pair of stands with forked tops upon which to lower the bar is absolutely necessary if training alone. For fitness and stamina, the use of fast repetitions of light weights is required. For muscle bulking the weights should be heavier.

Weight training is difficult to understand if one thinks in terms of heavy and light weights. One sailor's heavy weight is another's light weight. For this reason we have to think of the weight as it applies to one person only. We do this by defining the weight in terms of how difficult it is for a given person to lift it. The definition is in terms of RM or Repetitions Maximum. One RM is the heaviest weight we can lift once only 'in good form'. That is it is a weight that is too heavy for us to lift a second time. In lifting it once only we do so in a controlled and non dangerous way. A five RM weight becomes one that we can lift five times in succession in good style but which is too heavy for us to lift six times yet lighter than the weight that we could only lift four times. The accent has to be on the 'in good form' so that we do not injure ourselves with the last lift.

On this scale, one person's 5 RM weight may be half of anothers, but both sailors know what degree of heaviness we are talking about if we say go and train with weight equivalent to 5 RM. In training for general fitness with weights we are thinking of weights of 10 RM or over (ie 10 RM weight or less, say 12 or 20 RM). In such

training it is conventional to lift 15 RM, for example, in a fairly rapid sequence; repeating the sequence several times.

In weight training, for muscle bulking, the weight limit is from 10 RM or less (10 RM weight or heavier). In this form of training the weight lifting sequence may be in steadily increasing degree of heaviness. That is from perhaps 10 RM weight to 8 RM to 6 RM; progressively to 4, 3, 2 and finally 1 RM. This being the heaviest weight that the sailor can manage to lift once in good form. It is usual to work upwards in weight, lifting more each time. If you start by lifting your 1 RM maximum you may not be in good enough shape to progress downwards in weight!

Of course to determine your RM you have to try a maximum lift to start with. *Don't be too ambitious. Do not injure yourself. Do the lifts under supervision.* If your selected 1 RM maximum is in fact 3 RM there is no problem; as you improve, your RM will have to be re-adjusted anyway. At the end of three months' training, it is likely that you will be lifting a lot more than on the first week. This is partly due to the acquisition of skill in the task, partly to your learning to recruit more muscle fibres in a given muscle during the lift, and partly due to your having achieved your aim of making a stronger and more bulky muscle. Thus every few weeks the heavy and the light weight trainers have to redefine their RM so that they are still on the effective side of the dividing line for their chosen weight training routine.

Balanced training

Remember that every muscle has an 'opposite number' which is the muscle which works against the one you are training. If you seek to build up your quads on the front of the thigh, which are the extenders of the knee joint, remember the hamstrings which, at the back of the thigh, act as knee flexors. If the hams fall more than 60% behind the quads in strength there is every chance that you will 'pull' a hamstring muscle. This same logic will apply to all muscle groups. Sailing in a dinghy is very much a sport which places stress upon (and thus develops) muscles on the front of the body. The sailing position in the semi-hike is interesting in that if a photo of the sailor is rotated 90° so that the feet are on the ground, as opposed to being in mid air hanging on the straps, the posture is that of a bent old man or woman walking with the aid of a stick (tiller extension)!

When devising your muscle training programme therefore think in terms of a balanced development. Also make sure that you stretch these wonderful new muscle fibres that have been so hard won, since a well-stretched developed muscle will be of more use to you than one which is so tense that the joint which it controls now has a limited range of movement.

Lightweight fast repetitions tend not to increase muscle bulk, but will improve muscle tone and capillary circulation so that the blood supply improves, and the muscles are more efficient. Heavyweight training and prolonged isometric work will produce a more bulky muscle which is more powerful. It has been suggested however, that this results in a bulky heart muscle and raises blood pressure.

Common sailing injuries and their prevention

Competitive water sports are the cause of few injuries overall – less than two per cent in one study at an inland hospital. However, unaccustomed exercise is said to be occasionally fatal, frequently injurious and always painful!

Skill is paramount in safety. This involves physical control, an ability to read the situation, assess risk and know how to offset it and to be able to take necessary action. Sailors must, therefore, develop effective and efficient movement patterns, which should become conditioned reflexes.

The sailor is made vulnerable by fatigue and by nervous tension. The beginner or unskilled is especially open to injury both to himself and to other people. In addition, skill will not protect against conditions arising from over-exertion if the sailor pushes himself beyond the protection afforded by his own level of fitness.

Causes of sailing injuries

A survey of sailing injuries in the UK by Dr Newton printed in *The Physician* (August 1984) showed the following injuries: the back, 35%; head, 25%; knees, 20%; shoulders, 4% and finally elbows, 5%. The ankle is not prone to frequent injury in sailing due to the fact that the leg is not in motion as often, or as violently, as in some sports.

In terms of treatment, there is nothing specific to a sailing injury that makes it different when it has occurred to the same injury sustained in another sport or in a domestic or road accident.

Sports injuries occur more frequently both at the start of the competitive season, when the athlete is unfit, and at the end of the season when the athlete is tired by a long period of competition. In sailing, the time for injury may be the annual class championships spread over a week of tiring, back-to-back competition, combined with a social programme which may damage co-ordination and lead to injury.

In a single race, the time of greatest risk is at the start – before the athlete is properly warmed, particularly muscle elasticity, and near the end of a race when the muscles are fatigued by an accumulation of waste products that inhibit normal function, and particularly in sailing, by cold and ischaemia (poor circulation).

Optimum conditions are needed for effective body function be this internal (for example digestion) or musculo-skeletal for movement. The body core temperature is maintained within narrow limits and muscular contraction and relaxation in response to a command from the brain will be faster and more complete if the muscle is at the correct temperature. Having contracted, the muscle will relax in preparation for the next contraction at a faster rate if warmed up, than if it is cold.

Taking two opposing muscle groups: if one is cold and one is warm, there is a risk of an unco-ordinated contraction which may cause muscle injury. The rate of recovery of a fatigued muscle will depend upon blood circulation, temperature and supply of correct nutritional factors from the blood. This in turn requires the right food input at the correct time and in adequate quantity.

Muscle tissue itself varies in type for different tasks in the body. For example in a chicken, which mainly walks or runs we find darker muscle fibres in the legs, and pale meat in the breast, whereas in the pheasant, the 'fast' contracting flying muscles of the breast are dark fibres. The particular fibre mix in each individual is ordained by his or her genes. It follows that it is not always possible to make oneself a champion in certain sports unless the right muscle configuration has been inherited! However, in a sport like sailing, this should not prevent the well trained from reaching the top.

The available range of movement is an important factor in injury. In body contact sports, like rugby, or wrestling or American football, the risk to a limb or joint is considerable, if full flexion and extension are limited. The risk in sailing is not so great but the ability to sail may well be greatly reduced if the sailor has a limited range of movement. Factors limiting the range of movement include:

- Age, with early osteo-arthritic joint changes.

- Pre-existing injury with old scar tissue in muscles.
- Restrictive clothing, wet suits, life jackets and trapeze harness which limit full movement.
- Available room in the boat, eg boom clearance.

Avoiding injuries to the lower back

The lumbar spine is one of nature's grey areas. There seems to have been no set human design; there are a number of recognised variables. It does not follow, however, that a back with an unusual configuration is a painful or unstable back, and it certainly does not follow that if a lumbar spine is seen on an x-ray to be normal, it will be trouble free. X-rays show only bone structures; the trouble often lies in the associated discs, ligaments and joints.

Pain is the key word in relation to back problems. Back-pain may be accompanied by pain extending to the buttocks or down the thigh, often as far as the calf or foot. There may be loss of tendon reflex; loss of sensation of touch; sensations of pins and needles may occur; and significant wasting of muscle bulk. A sailor with such symptoms should not be allowed to sail until passed fit. These symptoms are caused by pressure on a spinal nerve or nerve root. Undue flexion, extension, rotation or tilt of the spine may increase this effect.

The use of the weight jacket should not be encouraged and its use is now prohibited in youth sailing. Loading of the spine produces 'creep effects' – the spine stiffens and is less capable of absorbing shocks. Compression of the spine can cause damage to discs and can even cause you to shrink! Loss of vertebral height has been recorded in healthy young adult males after loading the shoulders for 20 minutes with only 9 kg (Fitzgerald 1972). Creep effects are accelerated if the loaded spine is then exposed to vibration, known as the 'Vibro Creep Phenomenon'.

Conditioning factors making back injury more likely, are a prolonged state of static loading, vibratory stress, repetitive impacts and shocks. Individual capacity for spinal stress varies greatly depending upon size and physical characteristics of the vertebral column, muscular strength and skill, and on the presence or absence of degenerative changes and other abnormalities.

People suffering from chronic low back pain need to learn how to lift properly using their legs and avoiding strain on the back. This means being careful when launching and recovering a dinghy. Also, when hauling on sheets in the boat, it is possible to help preserve the back by extending the legs to assist pulling. A firm bed for sleeping, correct car seating and correct sitting posture also helps. Frequently, pain in the lower back is associated with tight hamstring muscles, so stretching of these can help.

Certain low spine problems are caused by undue mobility of the lumbar vertebrae, which enables them to slip forward, thus trapping the nerves. Such conditions may be helped by a supporting belt or corset. A neoprene belt worn when sailing should be worn over other clothing and have velcro adjustment.

Scheuermann's disease is a common condition caused by a growth disturbance occurring in the adolescent spine. In this condition the back is often noticeably rounded. Undue flexion of the back during growth is to be avoided if there is pain associated with such rounding. Careful choice of boat may be of help – choose one which your body weight can handle in the mid-upper wind range. Playing in the second row of the scrum is not advised either!

Neck injuries

The cervical spine (neck area) is a very mobile portion of the back and the head is a very heavy organ. The neck often shows signs of undue early wear and tear, or damage from injury in other sports or accidents. Pain from the neck may extend down the arms. Older sailors with neck problems may find difficulty in scanning the water, looking up to the rig, tell-tales or masthead indicators.

Head injuries

It may seem obvious that head injuries should have been near the top of the list in the census. However, to those injured, the mechanism of injury is not always that obvious. In sailing the call of 'lee oh' or 'gybe oh' is used as a warning. This call is often not used by a practised crew sailing together all the time, and a newcomer may be caught unawares and hit on the head. Particular care must be taken, therefore, in coaching those who are hard of hearing or who are deaf or blind. Helmets are seldom used in sailing but regularly in canoeing. They should be considered for windsurfers, for learner dinghy sailors and for those who have had a previous head injury. Some would say that they are worthwhile protection for all sailors who have the courage to wear them! The plastic type is inexpensive, adjusts to several sizes, and is light in weight.

In the event of a head injury, the coach should insist that the sailor takes no part in further sailing that day, as delayed onset of unconsciousness is not uncommon. The coach must be confident in resuscitation techniques and make sure that an airway is an essential part of his equipment. Remember that if a blow is hard enough to render a sailor unconscious, it may also have caused significant injury to the cervical spine. If the sailor is paralysed from the neck down and can't talk, then both sailor and coach are in serious trouble.

Knee injuries

The knee is potentially an unstable joint. To function properly, it requires good muscle tone in groups of muscles that cross the joint from above to below and vice versa. These pull the thigh bone (femur) and the shin bone (tibia) hard against each other, compressing the cartilages, which act as shims, between them. Angularity sideways is prevented by the inner (medial) ligament and the outer (lateral) ligament. Fore and aft movement is restricted by the cruciate ligaments inside the joint. They all work as a team.

Loss of function of part of the system can result in an unstable knee, which will rapidly become a painful, injured knee. It follows that, at all times, the muscles must be maintained in good tone with good bulk, and be well stretched.

In the event of a knee injury, a swelling of the joint occurring a day or so after the event probably indicates that fluid has seeped from bruised tissues. Rapid swelling within an hour or so may indicate bleeding within the joint. If bleeding is suspected, an immediate hospital opinion is essential as 75% of such cases have significant damage to internal structures.

Anterior knee pain

Some people suffer from pain behind the kneecap caused by its roughened under-surface grinding against the articular surface of the lower femur. This condition is found in those whose knees hyper-extend, and is common in children. During exercise with the knee bent, it has been suggested that a force as much as 10 times body weight may be applied through the knee. The stability of this joint will vary according to its degree of flexion.

In traditional hiking, as in the Finn dinghy, the (medial) inner quadriceps muscle is 'resting', while the main bulk of the other three quads is in sustained isometric contraction, therefore developing into a very strong muscle, which alters the dynamics of the joint. Anterior knee pain may become worse. In the Laser, the sustained, almost

straight leg sailing, will develop the medial quads and improve the condition. A third of the youth squad in winter training have this problem. After six weeks of isometric medial quads work, this is greatly reduced.

Ankle injuries

The ankle has not significantly featured as a structure in sailing injuries. It is not often injured in sailing but it is often injured in other activities that the sailor will be doing in training for sailing. The most common of the injuries is the inversion sprain when the foot is turned inwards awkwardly while it is carrying body weight. As a consequence, the ligaments on the outer side of the ankle joint are damaged. Swelling and bruising will occur, and on occasion the bone on one side or other of the joint may be fractured.

In the case of the sprain it is quite likely that the sailor will be advised to rest the part for too long. Too much rest may cause vital 'proprioceptive' function to be lost. This function keeps us aware of the position of our body in space, so that we may automatically make correct postural adjustments at once. Incorrect adjustment of the position of the ankle results in further injury. Practice with a 'wobble board' should start within 36 hours of the average ankle sprain, after observation of the ritual of initial ice, rest, compression and elevation (RICE). This rule also applies after a knee injury. As a substitute for the wobble board try a thick off-cut of upholstery foam, stand on it on the sprained ankle and swing the good leg slowly in all directions until the ankle feels secure.

The design of training shoes leaves much to be desired and helps cause ankle problems. High heel tabs found on most trainers are a cause of a soreness (peritendonitis) of the Achilles Tendon which can rapidly become a chronic condition. Frequent physiotherapy without correction of the shoes, is expensive and injurious to the tissues. Rugby boots, cricket boots and basketball boots may also cause similar problems.

Other injuries

Overuse injuries like tennis and golfer's elbow, are caused by poor technique. Over-gripping the tiller handle or the use of too small or too large a handle may cause problems. The grip should be light but firm. In boardsailing, pain in the forearm can be caused by too tight a grip upon the boom. Some top board sailors have suffered from compartmental compression of the circulation to forearm muscles, due to excessive development of these muscles within a limited space.

Many sailors in top competition take up running as part of their training and most find themselves running on road surfaces. Unlike athletes of the running world, they may not possess a good running gait, and if heavy-footed, may develop stress fractures. These may be prevented by the use of Sorbothane running shoe inserts made of a special compound which dissipates the force of impact in various directions, reducing the likelihood of stress fractures. It is available at good sport shops in the form of heel pads.

Gloves and suitable clothing are mandatory, particularly during winter training. Head covering greatly reduces heat loss. During cold winter training in Ireland, the grip strength of ten laser sailors was recorded before and after a one hour session on the water. A loss of up to 40 percent grip strength was noted in all but one sailor – the only girl. Females have better insulation than males due to thicker fat layers in the skin.

Risks to sailors

1 *Tetanus* It is advised that sailors be protected against tetanus which regularly causes death in the UK.

2 *Weil's Disease* This is a virus spread by the urine of infected rats. The risk is greatest in fresh water but can occur in the partly salty waters of estuaries. The virus enters the body through cuts, blisters and throat membranes. Wounds should be thoroughly washed and protected with fresh waterproof dressings. The disease starts as an illness with symptoms rather like 'flu', but jaundice may occur. All who sail where there is a known rat population should be warned to tell their doctors of the risk, if reporting sick with a flu-like illness. Weil's Disease is a medical emergency not to be treated over the phone with advice to take 'a couple of aspirin and two days in bed'. But unless advised of your sporting interest and risk, your doctor may reasonably assume if 'flu' is about that this is the cause of your illness.

3 *Sore throats and fevers* No athlete should be physically active when unwell for fear of the heart muscle being affected.

Psychology of the injury-prone athlete

The anxiety-prone athlete is also a loser in the sense of being more injury-prone. Some athletes find competitive sport so anxiety-inducing that they try to get over this by meeting it head on. Being overtly aggressive and fearless, such people tempt fate by testing their indestructibility, making them more prone to injury. They are attracted to high risk sports. An injury-prone hero sees his or her injury as a sign of strength and endurance and takes a martyr's role by continuing to compete despite his injury and secures admiration with a ready-made excuse.

In addition, a child who hates sport but cannot tell his parents, will use the threat of injury as a weapon, for example the young gymnast with 'backache' or the 'butterfly' swimmer with painful shoulders may be seeking an 'out' from a sport that they no longer enjoy. Also, there are competitors who fear competitions so much, that they need to be injured. When injured, they then avoid confrontation but can remain a member of the squad with their ego intact.

In a team sport their mates can use the injury as an excuse for their failure.

Sometimes injuries are psychological. There is no real hurt, but the sufferer is unreliable and may present his 'injury' at any time. In addition, an injury can be used to avoid training, because the person wishes to cause problems for his coach or for his team, or because he wishes to avoid unfavourable comparison with others.

Occasionally one comes across the anxious coach whose over-concern for an athlete's well-being which can, in turn, produce anxiety and tension in his athletes, who are then prone to injury.

Personality types have a lot to do with attitude to injury. Extroverts tend to be impulsive, optimistic with a high pain threshold and tend to ask 'When can I play again?' Whereas introverts tend to be apprehensive, have a low pain tolerance, overact and tend to ask 'Can I play again?' In addition, athletes are particularly vulnerable at a time when their overall athletic performance is in decline. After the age of 25 years, in many sports, we are in decline! Thank goodness in sailing there is usually a less demanding class to turn to!

Sod's syndrome

When all has been done that should have been done, then something will go wrong! In the case of sailors, a competitor will be injured by fooling about. This is most likely during the work up to an important event – probably when abroad when the sailor becomes bored with all day training and tuning prior to racing. The coach should be vigilant at all times of the day and night. A variety of non-standard training routines and diversions must be devised to combat boredom. It is essential that physical training is maintained, though the time of day may have to change. Also, athletes in training regularly secrete substances (endorphins) within their circulation to which they become 'addicted' and which gives them a

sense of euphoria or a 'high'. When they stop training, they miss these secretions and become moody and depressed. The time just before a competition is no time for a mood change.

Sailors should be aware, too, that progressive loss of muscle tone occurs rapidly especially after a long drive to a venue or when sleep is lost. The maintenance of a regular pattern of physical activity protects against mental stress. Prolonged periods in car, plane, coach etc., in a slumped sitting posture require corrective back extension routines before taking to the water.

Diet and the dinghy racer

Think of nutrition as six groups: *protein, fat* and *carbohydrate* (the bulk components) plus *minerals* (most of which are trace elements) *vitamins* and *water*. Stories circulate about the special benefits to be had from diets high in each one of these groups. Extra protein is said to build more muscle, extra fat is believed to keep your warm, 'carbohydrate loading' is claimed to give you endurance, others think the same about extra iron . . . and extra vitamins, well they are claimed to enhance every physical prowess there is! Let us look at each heading in turn.

Protein

You certainly don't need to eat 10 eggs and 3 lb of steak a day! The huge protein intakes of some athletes have little value except publicity. There is quite a lot of protein in wholemeal bread, vegetables (notably beans) and nuts; and, of course, there is a great deal in fish, yoghurt or cheese, and in milk. All of us like some of these foods, and many of us like all of them. So you can see that by eating a varied diet you should automatically eat enough protein, if you are a vegetarian. Only if you are a vegan – a vegetarian who abstains even from dairy products and eggs –

will you need to take extra care about getting sufficient protein. Probably the only other group today who may risk deficiency in the developed world are extremely faddy children but even here, a little extra of one protein source, milk for example, will compensate for the absence of others, such as meat and eggs.

Protein is not primarily a fuel, so it is not normally used up to provide energy. It is only needed to build or repair tissue. No adult who can afford a sport like sailing is likely to eat insufficient protein.

Fat

Eating extra fat is not the best way to keep yourself warm. If you have really become skinny, you can put on a bit of insulation (and energy reserve) just as effectively by eating carbohydrates, with less risk to your arteries in later life. The body is able to turn extra carbohydrate into fat, though it cannot turn extra fat into carbohydrate.

You certainly need some fat – partly for its own contribution to nutrition and partly for the vitamins it carries (see below). However, as with protein, it is hard *not* to take in all the fat you need. Not only do we spread it on bread and use it in baking, it is present in meat, eggs and unskimmed milk, as well as in nuts and chocolate and, of course, we fry things in it.

Carbohydrate

This is the main fuel food, so eat lots of it! Bread, cakes, all forms of cereals, fruit, beans and root vegetables, sugars, syrups and sweets – these are the principal carbohydrate foods. All give you energy, and none will make you fat as long as your energy output matches your intake. Stock up in advance, the meal before a big race should be particularly rich in carbohydrate. In addition if the race will be long, or there are to be two, back-to-back, take more carbohydrate-rich food with you in the boat.

A word of warning, however: there are two categories of carbohydrate – complex and simple. The simple carbohydrates are syrup and sugar, of which the simplest of all is glucose. The simpler the carbohydrate, the more rapidly it is absorbed by the body and the more rapidly it can be used. Take glucose in *small* doses (single tablets) every 20 minutes, or eat complex carbohydrates such as fruit, raw carrots, stuffed potatoes or filled rolls.

Carbohydrate loading

This technique, also called glycogen loading, was developed by Saltin in Sweden in the 1960s. It is well established for long-distance cyclists, swimmers and skiers, and is practised by many marathon runners. Now some sailors are trying it too. The full 'Saltin Diet' consists of training strenuously during the first half of the week before a big race, while eating a low carbohydrate diet. This exhausts the working muscles of their stocks of glycogen – the form in which they store carbohydrate. Then the athlete eats a high carbohydrate diet on the last three days before the race whilst performing light training. The ultra-hungry muscles grab all the carbohydrate they can during this time. By race day they may have twice the glycogen content they would have had if the usual ratio of eating to training had been maintained throughout that time. The consequence is that during the race the muscles not only work longer, but they do not compete so much with the brain for blood-borne sugar (glucose) so many athletes feel that their minds stay sharper too. The brain's only source of energy is the blood sugar. If this falls, then the brain is less effective in decision making.

The Full Glycogen Boost/'Saltin' diet is designed for endurance runners not sailors! However, there is an easier modified Glycogen Boost Diet which is quite suitable for sailors. This is to train as usual but to concentrate on a high carbohydrate intake in the three days before the regatta. In so doing, the exercise time to exhaustion will be significantly extended.

Do not forget that during exercise, the stores of glycogen are depleted in the exercising muscles, not in the ones that are having an easy time. Any new intake of glycogen is first deposited in the muscles that have been exercising, and is not shared out equally to every muscle in the body.

There will be some slight weight gain, as a result of carbohydrate loading, for either the full or the modified diet. Glycogen is stored with water in the body and is released following the demands of the exercise to fuel muscle work. In an endurance event this assists in combating dehydration, and it is possible that, in a marathon, the boost diet will benefit the body by preserving body fluid levels.

If, on the first day of a regatta the winds are light your glycogen stores will not be significantly depleted. However, if the winds are strong, you may score over those who arrived late at the event either having eaten little food, or lots of the wrong type in the preceding two days. The important point is that you start each day of racing with a high level of stored glycogen. If your energy stores become depleted you will still be better off than the competitor who starts with their stores low.

Body management

'Body management' has become an important part of many sports. We learn to 'manage' the dinghy by making adjustments to suit the prevailing conditions. We 'manage' the race strategy. We 'manage' the post race protest situation. We 'manage' the getting to and from the venue and we 'manage' the repairs required in the event of gear failure. Yet few give thought to assisting the body to manage. For some reason we expect it to do the job itself. In fact we often go out of our way to make the task more difficult by arriving tired, late and hungry at an important event.

Let us look at a few basic facts relating to diet and sport.

- Work requires energy which is derived from body stores. The first available source of energy is chemical and will not last the whole of a 100 metre race. Glycogen, stored in the muscles and liver, provides the next source of energy. The human energy balance is shown by:

$$\text{Body energy intake} = \\ \text{Body energy expended} \\ \pm \\ \text{Energy stored}$$

In other words, we may eat too little, too much or just enough for a particular task. Of the body's total energy intake, 60% is needed to 'run the body' while 10% is used for digestion.

- Extra carbohydrate, either complex or simple, eaten during the three days prior to a major event, may improve endurance capacity by up to 25%.
- Ideally, carbohydrate is taken as wholemeal bread, muesli, cereals, pasta, brown rice, fresh or dried fruit and vegetables, beans, peas, lentils and potatoes. These are unrefined complex carbohydrates. Cakes, biscuits and sweets should not provide the bulk of carbohydrate intake but are convenient and pleasant as booster snacks.
- When glycogen is burned in a working muscle, Lactic Acid (LA) is formed. Accumulating LA limits muscular work and LA is formed much earlier in an untrained than a trained person.
- The heart rate is lower on a high carbohydrate diet. Adrenaline levels are lower on a high carbohydrate diet.
- Most people eat too much fat. One-third of our food intake is generally in the form of snacks and, although you may not realise it, one-third of those snacks will be fat. If you are trying to reduce weight, reduce your fat intake, but you may have

	UK households Actual (1989)	COMA Recommended (1984)	LAUSANNE Sports people (1991)
Carbohydrate	45%	50%	60–70%
Fat	42%	35%	20–25%
Protein	13%	15%	10–15%

to increase your carbohydrate intake considerably to allow you to sustain training. When eating meat buy lean cuts, or cut out the fat.
• Alcohol significantly reduces the liver's capacity to re-synthesise glycogen.

A Sports Nutrition Symposium at Lausanne in 1991 noted the composition of diets (above).

An endurance athlete in training requires 10 grams Carbo per kilogram body weight per day and up to 1.5 grams Protein per kilogram plus some fat. Few sailors will require these quantities. But if you are very active at work and do other sports as well as sailing you may find that you will get tired unless you raise your carbohydrate intake.

A tired athlete cannot train. The body is too busy coping with its problems to spare the energy required for 'adaptation', which is what your training is all about.

Anorexia

There exists a condition known as post-exercise anorexia, or loss of a wish to eat, which prevents the early intake of further carbohydrate after a sports event. This is important especially to sailors who are competing in a series because they lose the opportunity to immediately 'top up' their glycogen levels. There is a phase of accelerated replenishment in the first hours after exercise which then falls significantly. So if you eat nothing for several hours after your race, it is impossible to get your stores back to normal in 24 hours. The eventual outcome is that towards the end of a week of heavy weather sailing you are going on to

the water with energy stores maybe only two-thirds of what they were on the first day of racing. Bearing in mind that you have trained hard for the event and are in top physical condition, having spent many hours in general fitness and on the hiking bench, it seems a pity that you throw the series for want of better 'body management'!

Refuelling

Feeding after the event must start at once. If the course is a long way from the shore you must take food with you rather than lose the early hours of rapid glycogen replacement.

This is illustrated in the diagram taken from the excellent publication *Nutrition for Sport* by Steve Wooton (Simon & Schuster):

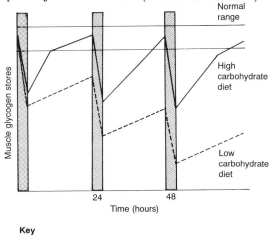

The effect of different amounts of carbohydrate in the diet on the refuelling of muscle glycogen following three bouts of exercise within a 72-hour period. There is a significant difference between the rate of refuelling on a high carbohydrate diet and one that is insufficient in carbohydrate.

Vitamin requirements of the athlete, sailor or otherwise, are adequately provided by the average diet. Scientific papers abound which, from time to time, advise extra of one or another vitamin but in most circumstances enough is enough. Remember that some vitamins are dissolved in fat and some in water. Those in water may be stored in the body less efficiently, as is the case with vitamin C. However, the sailors that this book is written for are unlikely to suffer from scurvy as in Nelson's day!

Mineral requirements are also provided in the average diet, though in young female (sailing) athletes there may be a requirement for extra iron and calcium. Remember that there is some extra value in the type of iron found in lean beef, fish and chicken meats. This is 'haem iron', which is a little different to the mineral iron found in iron tablets. Whilst there is adequate calcium found in a pint of milk per day this is, of course, fatty. Female athletes are advised to drink a pint of skimmed milk daily which will provide the calcium without adding extra fat to their diet. It is not advised that sailing or indeed any other athletes should take daily iron tablets without their doctor's approval.

It is often stated that in the UK sailing climate, extra salt is unnecessary because it is often cold and so there will be less likelihood of undue sweating and consequent fluid/salt loss. We have, however, progressed from wearing shirts and shorts to remarkable thermally-efficient sailing clothing. The micro-climate between the skin and the wet suit, dry suit or thermal longjohns etc is the climate that matters. Thus on a cold day we can still suffer from heat exhaustion if sailing hard in a strong wind and unable to ventilate the protective layers. We can lose much body fluid and some electrolytes, so you should drink one of the many iso-tomic drinks that are on the market. If that evening you feel the urge for a little extra salt on the tuna salad, it is probably because you need it.

Fluid levels are critical for performance in all active sports. Of our body weight, 70% is composed of water; 50% of this is in the tissue cells, 15% in the spaces between the cells and 5% in the blood. The fluid compartments are interchangeable. They can allow for six pints of beer in, or six pints of sweat out. We can sweat three pints per hour. If we sweat a lot and do not replace the fluid, dehydration leads to an increased heart rate, making us begin to feel distressed sooner. This water loss is also associated with a rise in body temperature of nearly 1°C. We then begin to suffer distress from overheating.

Sailing Championship competitors are advised to weigh themselves night and morning. A loss of one kilogram of weight is equal to one litre of fluid. This has to be replaced. Remember that thirst is a *late* symptom of dehydration. By the time you feel thirsty you are already dehydrated, your pulse is rising and your body is ill-equipped to handle the stress of competition. The sailor-athlete requires one litre of water a day to efficiently run the body. Plus an extra litre for every hour of training or competition. Sailors may not be endurance athletes but in their protective clothing they are susceptible to considerable fluid loss especially on a hot day. The answer is to drink as much water as you can to counter dehydration.

Fortunately, both our carbohydrate and our water requirements can be solved by the use of glucose polymer drinks. These contain long chain molecules of carbohydrate that do not taste sweet like sugar – an important factor when you are feeling thirsty. The carbohydrate and water are absorbed by the stomach and rapidly distributed round the body. The drink should be made up in weaker dilutions in hot weather, but stronger in cold weather when extra energy is needed. A 250 gram container of dry glucose polymer powder such as Caloreen (Roussel) would make

Strengths of carbo drinks in relation to climate	
Atmospheric temperature	% of carbo in drinks
Hot/warm 28°C	2%
Humid 25°C	4%
Warm 20°C	8–10%
Moderate/cold 20°C	12–14%

- In warm humid conditions, drinks should contain less carbo powder.

- In cold weather training, the concentration of powder may be increased to provide more energy.

- You should experiment to see what dilution suits you best in certain conditions.

- Plain water will not be absorbed as quickly as the carbo drinks. If you mainly need fluid replacement, use 5% powder to water.

many drinks and is far less expensive than the ready-made flavoured sports drinks.

Weight reduction

If you are trying to reduce weight, do not do this before a major event as it may affect your mood. Research has shown that when trying to train and compete whilst losing weight, the athlete may become more depressed, angry and tired. If you are training and working physically hard, as well as sailing, and you find that your weight is falling and you are tired, it is probably because your carbohydrate intake is too low. Increase it and see if your weight stabilises and your vigour returns. If it doesn't you may be over-training. Take a complete rest from training and sailing for a week before you begin again with a modified programme.

Recovery from exercise

As we already know, muscle glycogen is restored after 24 hours of recovery only if you start soon enough. Liquid and solid carbohydrates are equally effective over the first five hours of recovery. If you don't feel hungry after a race, take the carbohydrate as

glucose polymer liquid – one gram of polymer per kilogram of body weight immediately after exercise. Then repeat every two hours for up to six hours. Use simple sugars (sweets, cakes or biscuits) to supplement carbohydrate intake if you don't feel like eating a bulky, unrefined carbohydrate meal.

Don't sail for an hour back to shore, fill in a protest form, chat with friends, go for random sail measurement etc and *then* have your first food, several hours after the race has ended. If you do you are already a loser in the energy stakes for the race next day.

Psychological approach

Do we really need to incorporate psychology in our training programmes in order to win world titles when we have already won many major titles over the years without it? Much is said about this subject, of which some is beneficial and some is rubbish. However, in my opinion, psychology is good in our sport only for those who really need it. Those individuals who feel it is not really necessary for them should leave it well alone – so decide where you stand on the issue.

Some coaches do consider that psychological warfare exists in our sport in some events. For example, they will endeavour to keep their teams away from their opponents or from being upset or worried. Likewise, competitors are kept away from the media or from what they might read in the national press either about themselves or the opposition which, in any case, would probably be totally misleading.

I believe that preparation is two-thirds of the battle. If you have prepared yourself properly for your event in every respect you will already have a psychological advantage. *Remember only the fittest, both physically and mentally will win*. By preparing properly you can help yourself to think positively and be confident that you can do well. This will be possible if you have thoroughly completed your training programme for the event covering all aspects of the sport. Believe in your own ability – you *are* good enough and you *can* do well. Confidence breeds more confidence. However, never *expect* to win or do well because if you do you will only become over-confident and probably fail.

To be successful you must have a positive attitude and positive thinking supported by:

- Motivation
- Commitment
- Determination
- Controlled aggression
- Confidence

Think of your mind as a parachute – it will only work whilst it is 'open' and this means both in the boat and also on shore. Anxiety is a problem here which may be caused by a variety of things, pressure, nerves, arousal, perhaps related to an increase in heart rate due to good or bad expectations. Because of nervousness in facing certain opponents you may develop defensive behaviour – this must be overcome. Nerves undermine self-confidence and your mind closes, you must keep your self-confidence at all times even if your results are poor. *Never give up.*

As the reverse of positive thinking, *negative* thinking brings *negative* results. Negative thoughts can be brought on by:

- Too much sailing
- Too much training
- Emotional stress
- Illness

Do not be afraid to lose but *fight* to win. You may like to try mental exercises to assist in the reduction of negative thoughts an anxiety such as thinking to yourself:

- I feel very calm
- I feel completely relaxed
- I am breathing deeply and calmly
- My heart-rate is normal

Ambitions, aims, objectives

Once you have decided what your ambitions are (either short, medium or long-term), you must form a plan. This plan will be aiming at the event in which you wish to do well, and will primarily include your training programme both on and off the water. Training will cover a minimum period of four months for a major dinghy event and longer for a large keep boat event. Having completed this programme covering all aspects of the sport, plus your organisation/administration for the event concerned, you are now psychologically in a good frame of mind to proceed into a successful championship.

In terms of performance you should look within yourself and consider the following components:

- Nutrition
- Fitness
- Skills
- Psychology

With the correct nutrition you can become fit, when fit you can improve your skills, when skills are at their best then psychologically you are on top of your game. Without these foundations you cannot be successful. These four headings are the basis of self-confidence, and please remember that self-confidence can only be built upon in a positive atmosphere with positive thinking. Likewise, emotionally you must be on the

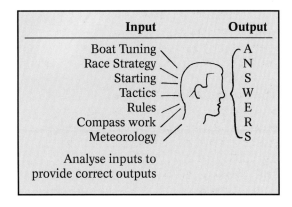

Input	Output
Boat Tuning	A
Race Strategy	N
Starting	S
Tactics	W
Rules	E
Compass work	R
Meteorology	S

Analyse inputs to provide correct outputs

offensive with an attitude of attack – a 'go for it' frame of mind for the task in hand. You must have the will-power to win and to do well both in your training and in competition. Warm up ashore and afloat – this will help you to relax; stand up in the boat doing some deep breathing exercises during the final ten minute period to assist in reducing anxiety levels.

There is a variety of obstacles involved in setting ambitions. These are summarised under the following headings:

- Time
- Money
- Motivation
- Determination

- Skill level
- Realism
- Physical compatibility
- Gamesmanship
- Sportsmanship

Remember, when sailing two-handed machines, two computers are better than one!

Above all, *enjoy* your sailing first and foremost. Improving your performance should be your second priority. You can achieve this by being self-critical, working on your weaknesses in more detail both in practical and theoretical areas. Train regularly, focusing on specifics. Establish *how* to win, not *what* to win.

3

Boat Preparation

For many boating spouses, the most dreaded words are 'boat preparation'! As far as they are concerned, this means that their partner heads for the garage, not to be seen until hours later! Yet boat preparation must be high on the list of priorities during training and championship preparation for the sailor who wishes to win races. The boat must be ready for (and survive) the event, or all other preparations will have counted for nothing. Boat preparation requires total commitment – not only leading up to the event, but also during it.

Strict one-design classes such as the Topper and Laser that use standard kit have far fewer problems than those that are not so one-design governed and can choose their equipment and materials, looking for extra speed and pointing ability. These are more the development classes that are not strictly one-design, as they work within tolerances that can make hulls, spars, sails and foils very different.

Whether you are racing a strictly one-design class or a development class boat, the basic theory of boat preparation still applies, because you must survive every race across the wind range. It is equally important that your boat and equipment meet measurement requirements. Measurement of each boat takes place before a championship event, and you do not need the aggravation of failing (and subsequently spending valuable time correcting the problem) when you could be on the water training – or even just relaxing.

Racing Rule 20 makes it quite clear that, when applicable (for development classes in particular), a valid measurement or rating certificate is required; and this must be produced at registration prior to the event. Surprisingly, competitors still arrive at events without the necessary documentation and wonder why their entries are refused. However, it is worth noting that competitors can still sail in the event if they can produce a certificate, or copy, during the event (Rule 20.3(a)). This Rule 20 is a very important part of your boat preparation regime and must not be forgotten. Measurement and the legality of a racing machine is the owner's responsibility at all times.

At most national and international events, the measurement team will carry out spot checks both on and off the water throughout the event, so you need to be sure of your vessel at all times. The most common problems over measurement are:

Hull – underweight
Spars – black bands in the wrong place or missing
Sails – numbers in the wrong place, or sailmaker's emblem too large and/or in the wrong place
Foils – too thick, too thin, too heavy, too light or illegal materials
Fittings – in the wrong place

Before going to an event, all the above points should be checked and any problems dealt with.

Preparing a racing machine for an important event involves many different areas that can be approached in the following order:

Boat preparation must be 101% to survive the race. Gear failure at the top level of competition in any class is unthinkable – check everything thoroughly and regularly.

Hull: outer finish, stiffness, weight

The outer hull must be fair and have a racing finish. It is no good arriving at a high-level championship event with a hull that is dirty, scratched and chipped, or with protruding screw heads or with slot gaskets and self bailers not faired in, and then wonder why boat speed is below par! The outer hull should be cleaned with fine abrasive polish to produce a slightly dulled matt finish to reduce the surface drag and allow for better water-to-hull separation.

Today's boat manufacturers are using more advanced materials and superior building techniques to produce stiffer boats that last much longer than previously. This is good news for competitors, but unfortunately

such boats do not last for ever – especially if they are not looked after and transported carefully to and from events. It is important to take care of the hull and its stiffness. Check it frequently by turning it upside down or on its side and, using the ball of your hand, try pushing in the hull around the area of the mast, back to the after end of the centreboard case where it is going to take the pounding on the waves. If it has gone soft in this area, it is time to change as performance will have been lost. However, softness is not a problem in the stem and stern areas, where the boat is lighter.

The boat's weight is obviously fairly critical, especially in performance dinghies, and it is important to try to keep the boat down to near minimum weight. This is not normally a problem. It is advisable whenever possible, perhaps during the winter months, to air out your boat with the aid of a heater or a light bulb let into the side tanks or forward hatch. Do not arrive at an event with a boat that is underweight and that already has maximum allowed correctors fitted! If you do, you will definitely have a problem bringing it up to weight.

Spars

In strictly one-design classes, all spars are supplied by the one manufacturer and should therefore be identical. However, even here, all-up weights have been found to be different, resulting in lighter, softer, heavier or stiffer spars. So if you are a lightweight helm and/or crew, if possible try to acquire the lighter, softer, more bendy spar; and vice versa for heavier weights.

In the development classes, 'the world's your oyster'. What are *your* specific requirements? Ask yourself the following questions:

- How much will it cost?
- Which manufacturer?
- Which section?
- Stiff mast sideways and fore-and-aft?
- Soft mast sideways and fore-and-aft?
- What is our all-up bodyweight?
- Flat or choppy water venue?
- Flat or full mainsail?
- What is the class World Champion/ National Champion using?

Once you have answered all these questions, you will be able to reach a decision. You may even decide on a mast for flat water venues and one for the open sea – if allowed in your class rules (and your budget!). Below is a guide to the various mast sections and data to help you select the most suitable mast.

Super spars mast selection

The correct choice of Super Spars for any particular class is determined by the bend characteristic you require, relative to the smallest section (for minimum windage), and minimum weight. You will need to take account of your sail shape and crew weight when making your spar selection and if

there is any doubt seek advice. See table for size, weight and stiffness.

M1 is a flexible and light mast in the range. It is ideal for smaller dinghies and is very successful in National 12s, Cherubs, Gulls, Graduates, Solos, etc.

M2 is the real powerhouse combining lightweight and stiffness to produce a moderately stiff rig for most medium-size dinghies. This is already a very successful design for Javelins, Flying Fifteens, 505s and many other classes.

M3 has the same stiffness sideways as M2, but is more flexible fore-and-aft.

M4 is designed for classes requiring an all-round, stiffer-than-average spar, and is

MAST DIMENSIONS

Section	Size (mm)	Weight (Kg /m)	Stiffness
M1	55 x 68	0.94	34
M2	57 x 72	1.05	44
M3	57 x 68	1.04	40
M4	57 x 72	1.15	47
M5	57 x 72	1.21	49
M6	61 x 74	1.19	55
M7	57 x 69	0.95	42
M8	55 x 69	1.14	44
M9	53 x 64	0.90	28

BOOM DIMENSIONS

Section	Size (mm)	Weight (kg/m)
B1	60 x 72	1.03
B2	60 x 82	1.08
B3	60 x 67	0.98
B4	76 x 76	1.05

Proctor's Mast Selection

Mast Sections		Weight (kgs/mt)	A (mm)	B (mm)	Fore & Aft Stiffness	Sideways Stiffness
2420		0.78	61	50	10.0	7.5
Lambda		0.86	63	51	13.0	10.0
C		0.90	65	54	14.0	10.0
Kappa		0.91	67	55	16.5	12.0
D		0.97	73	57	19.5	12.0
Stratus		0.98	69	57	19.5	15.0
Epsilon		1.02	72	57	20..0	15.5
D+		1.03	73	57	19.5	14.0
Nimbus		1.16	68	54	20.0	15.5
E		1.17	70	54	19.0	14.0
Cirrus		1.2	75	65	28.0	20.0
Gamma		1.22	75	56	27.0	16.0
F		1.35	78	60	30.0	20.0
Electron		1.00	61	66	11.0	18.0
Zeta		2.20	85	65	31.0	41.0

Boom Sections

2520		1.06	63	53	20.0	11.0
2628		1.00	72	63	26.0	16.0
2229		1.05	75	55	30.0	14.0
2633		1.06	85	66	40.0	18.0

suitable for all boats needing a slightly stiffer spar than M2.

M5 is the ultimate, no-compromise Flying Dutchman spar.

M6 has swept the board in the International 14 fleet where it is proving to have just the right combination of strength, stiffness and light weight for this most demanding class. It is also ideally suited to large dinghies such as the Laser 16, small cruisers and even Micro Cuppers.

M7 is the new Super Spars section developed for the 1990s. Its low weight coupled with excellent sideways stiffness and medium fore-and-aft stiffness, produces a spar of outstanding performance potential, improving on the concept developed by the M3 to produce a spar with the optimum dynamic response required to match modern dinghy sails.

M8 has been developed as a more flexible Flying Dutchman mast.

M9 is the smallest lightweight section for use on Youth Trainer boats, eg the 405 and 370.

Sails

Again, one-design classes have no choice; the sails are all supplied by the same manufacturer using the same weight of cloth and the only difference is how the sails are set up. For the development classes, there are yet another set of questions:

- Which sailmaker?
- What will the cost be?
- Flat water venue? If so, flatter sails/firmer leeches.
- Choppy water venue? If so, fuller sails/softer leeches.
- What mast? The mainsail luff curve needs to be matched to the bending characteristics of the mast to produce optimum shape and performance.
- What is the class World Champion/ National Champion using?

When you have gathered all the necessary information, take it to your chosen sailmaker. You may well find that they are currently carrying out research and development in your particular class of boat. Ideally, try to use a sailmaker whose loft is situated close to you, so that you can develop a good relationship and visit the loft to discuss ideas and information. If possible, watch the sail being made – that way, you could learn a lot about your sails.

Foils

Here, technology has advanced enormously in terms of both design and materials. Keels, centreboards and rudders have, in recent years, been seen in various shapes and sizes. A variety of different materials are now being used, either throughout the foil or trailing or leading edges only, or a different material is used in the top section to that in the bottom section.

Once again, strictly one-design classes use a standard design and materials, whereas in the development classes there is much to be gained by having good foils. Look at what the top sailors are using; visit the top foil manufacturers and decide on the best shape and materials allowed in your class rules. When you have acquired your foils, make sure that they are finished off in the same way as your hull finish so that foils and hull become the same through the water.

Most sailors will, if their class rules allow, look for a maximum weight keel/centreboard and a minimum weight rudder blade in order to bring the boat up to weight

Having selected your sails, look after them and make sure that they are properly packed and ready for setting!

and at the same time keep the centre of gravity of the boat as low as possible. However, it is important not to have the rudder blade so light that it snaps in the upper wind/sea state on a reach! Most under-canvased boats will go for a centreboard that is very stiff sideways for good pointing ability, whereas the over-canvased boats will prefer something softer in the mid to upper wind range, assisting the depowering of the boat and reducing weather helm, especially – if class rules permit – in the upper part of the board: stiff sideways, softer bottom sideways.

Centreboards and rudder blades are very expensive items and need to be looked after. When they are not in use, make sure that they are put in their bags or that, when left in the boat, the trailing edges of centreboards are protected. When visiting the hotter climates, do not leave them lying in the sun as they can easily twist, warp and even swell, and could therefore fail measurement. If this does happen, find a deep freezer to leave them in for an hour or so!

Fittings

There are numerous fittings to choose from, and which ones you finally acquire depends upon your personal budget. As a guideline, you should try to use as few as possible to reduce:

- Your overall budget
- All-up weight of the boat
- Risk of gear failure

Wherever possible, make sure that all fittings are bolted on so that they cannot pull out. Also, make sure that after each day of use they are thoroughly washed in fresh water to get rid of any salt, sand, grit and dirt – especially all blocks and cleats. Maintenance of a boat will vary depending on how big the vessel is and how much equipment is on board. For example, maintaining an International 14 may take eight hours a week, whereas a Laser 1 may only take eight minutes!

Boat layouts can go from one extreme to the other in some classes: some with very few fittings, others a mass of rope, blocks and cleats. Try to keep your boat as simple as possible for the reasons already mentioned.

There are some ingenious systems to operate all the boat tuning controls in the development classes, and it is well worth spending some time at dinghy exhibitions, boat shows or in the dinghy parks at international events studying these systems to pick up good ideas – and even to better them.

Boat preparation is an on-going subject because ideas and fashion change with the developments in technology, materials and designs. You must always keep abreast of these developments if you are to stay at the front of the fleet.

For the upper wind range and sea state all
fittings; spars; sails; ropes and wires in any
class of boat must be able to withstand the
stresses and strains which are placed upon
them.

4

Boat Handling

To many sailors, the subject of boat handling may seem trivial when compared to the other aspects of the sport. How wrong they are! Boat handling is given a high priority within a good training programme, as this subject alone can be the winning or losing factor in all weather conditions.

Both helm and crew must concentrate fully on their boat handling skills on all points of sailing, for both boat balance and boat trim can affect boat speed, pointing ability, stability and steerageway. Incorrect boat balance, boat trim and sail trim are the causes of instability and loss of steerageway, especially off the wind. Members of the crew who are trimming the sails and those who are acting as ballast must always concentrate on giving the helmsman a neutral helm the

It happens to all of us! The point here is to make sure you practise your righting drill during your training programme. There is a correct, quick way to right any boat and one

day you will find that whoever can right their boat the quickest will probably go on to win the race and even the championship. It has happened before!

whole time. As soon as the helmsman needs to use the helm it creates drag and slows down the boat. Ensuring that the helmsman has a neutral helm is always down to the crew, as a whole, giving it to him through boat balance/trim and sail trim, and it cannot be stressed enough that these factors require maximum concentration on any point of sailing. Points to work on are:

- Boat balance (athwartships)
- Boat trim (fore-and-aft)
- Sail trim (point of sailing)
- Tacking (roll)
- Gybing (roll)
- Spinnaker hoist
- Spinnaker gybe (reach to reach/run to run)
- Spinnaker drop
- Crewing
- Mark rounding

Boat balance and trim

Boat balance and trim are two of the most important boat handling disciplines on each point of sailing throughout the race in any racing machine. They are also the ones that are most often forgotten about! *Balance* (athwartships) and *trim* (fore/aft) require constant maximum concentration, especially in high-performance racing dinghies. This tends to be more often forgotten on the offwind legs of the course, especially when dead running in light airs. The same applies to the lighter displacement keel boats.

To windward (beating)

Light winds
Boat balance to leeward, boat trim forward. The amount varies from class to class depending on the underwater wetted area and shape of the boat. Balance to leeward in these conditions is primarily to let the sail(s) take their correct shape with the least amount of wind.

Medium wind range
Boat balance upright, boat trim to give maximum waterline length. Some high-performance dinghies require the boat balance slightly to windward to get the centre of effort of the rig directly above and slightly to windward of the centre of lateral resistance to neutralise the helm. This is very effective in the 420, 470 and 505.

Upper wind range
Boat balance should be as flat as possible, depowering the rig enough to achieve good boat balance whilst sailing to windward. Boat trim should be slightly further aft to assist raising the bow over the waves, which is especially critical on the open sea.

Reaching

Light winds
Boat balance to leeward to reduce the wetted area and assist in filling the sails with the least amount of wind, but on a broad reach with enough wind to fill the mainsail, then the boat should be balanced to windward (this is very rewarding in spinnaker boats!). In all cases, the boat trim should be forward.

Medium wind range
Boat balance upright for maximum power with boat trim giving maximum waterline length.

Upper wind range
Boat balance as flat as possible all the time. If over-powered in the doublehanders, ease the kicker more and raise the board more to assist in balance and stability. In the singlehanders, only ease the kicker slightly and play the mainsheet, as you luff in the lulls and bear away in the gusts. The boat trim should be further aft in order to raise the lee bow more readily off the water to enable the helm to bear away more easily in the gusts.

One slip with your foothold can potentially lead to disaster and most certainly lack of maximum power at a critical time, with too much boat balance to leeward. Ensure that your toe straps are a good fit and are not likely to break.

This helmslady must assist the crew by hiking out harder to correct the boat balance which is too much to leeward. If overpowered she would help by easing the mainsheet a little.

Running

Light winds

Boat balance to windward always, unless there is not enough wind to fill the mainsail, then to leeward. Boat trim should be forward for reasons already mentioned earlier.

Upper wind range

Boat balance slightly to windward for maximum power while dead running. Boat trim giving maximum waterline length.

Upper wind range

Boat balance upright and boat trim aft in order to raise the bow off the water, therefore reducing the risk of the 'death roll'! With the boat trim maximum aft and the boat dead upright, you will be quite safe dead running. To assist in reducing the 'death roll', ensure that the kicker is tensioned, the spinnaker is not allowed to come to windward too much, and that the spinnaker pole is kept low to flatten the spinnaker.

Sail trim

Since the sail is the powerhouse of the boat, total concentration is absolutely necessary for the whole time on each point of sailing. Using the telltales and, off the wind, the wind indicator; main, headsail and spinnaker trimmers are constantly adjusting sheets and boat tuning controls to maintain maximum boat speed and pointing ability across the wind range and sea state – also

Excellent concentration: looking for the waves and maximising speed during a reaching leg of the course. There is much to be gained or lost here by pure physical and mental effort without infringing Rule 54!

considering course and wind direction change. Good sail trim does require maximum concentration and should be given automatically without the helmsman having to call for it. Sail trim is also critical for boat handling manoeuvres. For example, when tacking, tension the mainsheet as you luff up to assist the speed of the turn off the mainsail leech and slightly ease the headsail – especially genoas in the middle to upper wind range. When bearing away, ditch the main rapidly, but keep the headsail over-trimmed to get the bow to pay off rapidly. Use the sails as much as possible, as well as boat balance, and trim to turn the boat and use less rudder which, after all, becomes a brake if overused. To learn more about sail trim combined with boat balance and trim, plus the overall characteristics of your boat,

find a clear patch of water, take off the rudder (or in a keel boat, lash it amidships), and sail the boat without the rudder on each point of sailing. It's very useful to have the practice – as one day you may have to do it for real in order to make it home.

Roll tacking

From an Optimist to a J24, this manoeuvre, if executed properly every time you tack, will gain you feet over those who do not get it right. The important factors for making a good roll tack are as follows:

1 sail trim
2 boat balance
3 not too much rudder
4 slightly backwind the headsail
5 bodyweight does not move across the

A good example of perfect boat balance, boat trim, sail trim and centreboard positioning, with the hull at maximum speed and the

mainsheet trimmed off the boom ready to respond to the next luff or to bear away on the waves.

Total concentration on board this Tornado maximising sail trim and use of the waves to maintain maximum speed.

boat until after the bow is through the eye of the wind

6 bodyweight moves together

7 main and headsail are brought in together as the boat is brought back upright

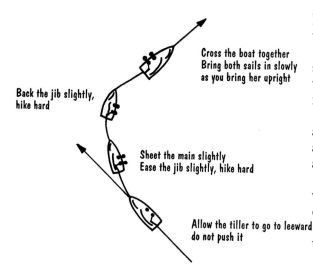

Cross the boat together
Bring both sails in slowly
as you bring her upright

Back the jib slightly, hike hard

Sheet the main slightly
Ease the jib slightly, hike hard

Allow the tiller to go to leeward do not push it

Roll gybing

To make a good roll gybe, the following points should be considered:

1 While bearing away you must ease the mainsail, especially in the mid to upper wind range, in order to reduce rudder angle to turn the boat (not so critical in light winds).

2 Balance the boat over to windward.

3 Trim the boat for maximum waterline length in light airs, further aft in stronger winds.

4 Do not use too much rudder; this will slow the turn down and could, in the upper wind range, stall out (especially small rudders, eg Lasers).

5 Look now for the mainsail leech to lift and signs of wanting to move. At this point, assist the mainsail across with the mainsheet and/or kicker.

6 Quickly move bodyweight to the new weather side and centralise the tiller as you cross the boat.

7 As you complete the gybe, be prepared to sheet the mainsail in if the boat rolls over

As the crew puts the pole on, the helm should be on his feet, tiller between his legs making sure that the spinnaker fills. Team work here gains metres over those who do not try.

to windward because of too much upper mainsail leech twist, especially in the upper wind range.

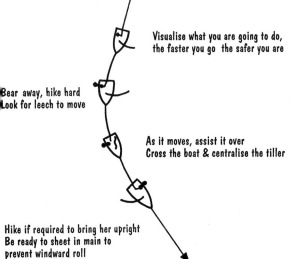

Visualise what you are going to do, the faster you go the safer you are

Bear away, hike hard
Look for leech to move

As it moves, assist it over
Cross the boat & centralise the tiller

Hike if required to bring her upright
Be ready to sheet in main to
prevent windward roll

Spinnaker hoisting

A good deal of ground can be gained or lost when it comes to hoisting the spinnaker – whether it is on to a reach or a run, a bear-away or gybe set, or a windward or leeward hoist. Important points to remember when hoisting the spinnaker in a bear-away hoist on to a reach when you are laying the windward mark are as follows:

1 Pole up before you get to the mark, guy in and up and downhaul set. In a trapezing dinghy, the helm does this while the crew steers from the wire using a telescopic tiller extension (class rules permitting).

2 Hoist the spinnaker as you pass the mark.

3 In breezy conditions, get off the wind and only come back on to course when ready to do so.

4 As the spinnaker is hoisted, the crew pulls round the guy and cleats it (this can be done by the helm if the crew stays out on the wire in very high-performance dinghies), and the spinnaker is sheeted and filled. The

Having born away, notice how the jib has been kept oversheeted so that, as the spinnaker is hoisted by the helm, it clears the jib with less friction and does not try to drag the jib up with it as it comes out of the leeward bag.

record time in which this has been done from passing the mark is three seconds; the average time is five to eight seconds.

5 In breezy conditions raise the centreboard first on passing the mark, especially if the crew has to come in for any reason; otherwise, you will broach and capsize.

Remember: If you hoist the spinnaker from the leeward side aft of the headsail, do not over-ease the headsail as you bear away. If you do, you will drag the headsail foot up with the spinnaker, creating a great deal of friction in the hoist.)

Windward hoisting
If and when you have to do a windward hoist, here are some important points to note:

1 Bear away to a broad reach/run.
2 Crew gathers spinnaker in one or both hands.
3 Helmsman calls; crew throws spinnaker both up and forward as the helmsman hoists.
4 Helmsman takes the guy and sheet while the crew does the pole.
5 Crew then takes the guy and cleats it off, then the sheet.
6 Helmsman takes the main and settles on the course.

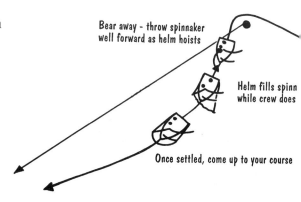

Bear away - throw spinnaker well forward as helm hoists

Helm fills spinn while crew does

Once settled, come up to your course

When carrying out a windward hoist, remember to get well off the wind for the hoist, otherwise you will find that the spinnaker passes between the mast and the forestay, creating more problems for both the helmsman and crew – in fact, you may even capsize.

Spinnaker gybing

Good spinnaker gybing is, as always, down to good team work. Your objective is to keep the spinnaker full throughout the gybing manoeuvre. This is quite easily done while executing the gybe from a run to a run, or broad reach to broad reach, and all efforts must be made to keep the spinnaker full to gain over those who do not.

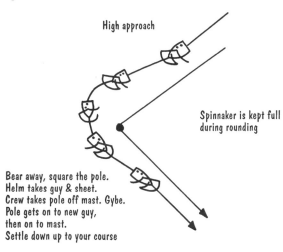

High approach

Spinnaker is kept full during rounding

Bear away, square the pole.
Helm takes guy & sheet.
Crew takes pole off mast. Gybe.
Pole gets on to new guy,
then on to mast.
Settle down up to your course

There are obviously times when it is not critical to keep the spinnaker full and pulling, but more important just to square it round and initially get high – for example, on a new reaching leg to gain the advantage tactically and/or defend your wind. In a doublehanded dinghy, the majority of helms are too lazy and do not do enough to help the crew execute a good spinnaker gybe. The most common faults are that the helmsmen do not stand up in the boat and take both the guy and sheet in hand to keep the spinnaker full while the crew does the

pole. Secondly, they do not steer the boat underneath the spinnaker while it is free floating with the tiller between their knees. Points to follow when spinnaker gybing:

1 Bear away and square the spinnaker.
2 The helm now stands, and takes both sheet and guy from the crew.
3 Crew takes the pole off the mast, passes it in front of the mast, leaving it on the uphaul/downhaul and the old guy.
4 The helm bears away and gybes, crew weight comes aft, and he assists the main over.
5 After the gybe, the crew has the end of the pole immediately in front of him and puts it on to the new guy from the old and on to the mast.
6 The crew then takes the guy, secures it, and takes the sheet from the helm who then takes the mainsheet.

By using the above method, you keep the crew away from the mast area after a gybe, which is critical in preventing a broach or capsize in the upper wind range.

Spinnaker drop

In high-performance dinghies that carry spinnaker bags, always take the spinnaker down to windward. It is critical for the crew to take the spinnaker down along its luff followed by the rest. This guarantees the spinnaker will not be twisted on the next hoist.

When dropping the spinnaker, you must do it so that you round the leeward mark close-hauled ready to go. Judge the speed of approach accurately, allowing for tide (if applicable) across the wind range. Important factors are:

• Communication
• Speed of approach
• Crew responsibilities
• Halyard free to run

Communication is the all-important point for the drop. The crew needs to know in

Whilst on a power reach it is important to make sure that the spinnaker pole is not allowed to rest on the forestay. The guy must be marked and cleated off to prevent this from happening, as shown here.

Overpowered on a reach? In any boat, ease the kicker tension to reduce the power of the mainsail leech and therefore the heeling moment of the boat. With the boom end in the water this normally ends up with the crew trying to use the mainsail as a trampoline!

good time which drop it is going to be: windward, leeward or float/gybe drop. Poor judgement of the boat's speed of approach to the mark is a common fault. In tidal conditions in a strong wind with the tide, the mark is more often than not overshot and undershot in light airs against the tide. Make sure that you judge both situations correctly.

Knowing who is going to do what during the manoeuvre is essential; otherwise, especially in keel boats or if several people are involved, any problem will just get worse. You must know who is going to look after halyard, guy, sheet and pole, and gather in the spinnaker. In dinghies with bags, make sure it is taken down correctly to

Spinnaker trimmers must be ready for this. As hull speed approaches the wind speed and apparent wind goes rapidly forward, so must the pole, and the spinnaker trimmer must rapidly sheet in to prevent the spinnaker from collapsing. However, he will not be able to trim the spinnaker when the hull speed overtakes the windspeed. Very exciting!

ensure that there is no twist on the next hoist. Also, make sure that the halyard is free to run; it may pay you to stream it astern prior to the drop to prevent any knots – especially in the upper wind range when there may be lots of water swilling around in the bottom of the boat, which may cause the halyard to become knotted.

Crewing

Good crews probably account for 70 per cent of a top team's success, and they deserve much more credit than they generally get. If you have a good crew, look after them, for they are worth their weight in beer! While racing, the helmsman must be allowed to concentrate on making the boat go as fast as possible, while the rest of the burden falls on the crew's shoulders. Crew and helmsman must know exactly which are their respective tasks on all points of sailing and in all wind strengths. Only a lot of hard training and time spent on the water together will produce the high standard

The 'eyes' on the weather rail will be calling the bigger waves approaching the weather bow and also letting the helmsman know the increase and decrease in wind velocity so that he and the trimmers can react accordingly.

necessary to win races at the top level of competitions. In the dinghy world, the crew needs to be very agile, sharp and have very quick reflexes; speed of reaction must be good. In addition, all movement must be very sensitive to the needs of the boat – particularly in the light to medium wind range. Many crews are far too aggressive with the boat and sails in light conditions when sensitivity and lightness of touch are so important. Remember, when racing to windward the crew will be the tactician of the boat, and in non-spinnaker boats they may also be the tactician off the wind.

Good crews tend to be very self-critical and analyse their weaknesses mainly through the use of video and working with a coach. Using video, crews can quickly digest and analyse techniques on tacking, gybing, spinnaker hoists and drops, and also mark-

rounding manoeuvres. On bigger boats, each crew member should know each other's job and what each one is going to do for every manoeuvre. A useful exercise during training is to write down exactly what you do during each manoeuvre and exchange notes with the rest of the crew. You will be surprised in the earlier part of your training programme how many other people are going for the same piece of rope!

Common crewing faults

The following are the most common faults of trapezing and non-trapezing crews:

- slow reactions
- facing forward while tacking (depending on layout of job sheets)
- trapezing crews – flat-footed on the gunwale with legs too far apart. Also, not using forward hand to support the head (preventing neckache) when on a long tack.

The following faults are not directly related

Here the bodyweight of both helm and crew is too far forward; both need to be further aft to lift the lee bow off the water more easily. The crew's after leg needs to be on the shoulder of the helm and she should be on her toes more for extra leverage.

to boat handling, but they are worth mentioning here:

- Lack of fitness.
- Not communicating with the helmsman on what is happening outside the boat.
- Clothing – not streamlined enough, thus offering too much wind resistance, bulky lifejackets and general lack of suitable clothing.

Solving these problems and learning the art and skill of crewing requires practice and experience, as well as patience on the part of the helmsman! If you are a helmsman, remember to take good care of your crews – after all, they do win the race by crossing the finishing line first!

Mark rounding

Many sailors have problems during a rounding manoeuvre, mostly because of poor skills in boat handling. The faults most often experienced are:

- Inability to bear away around the windward mark.
- Broaching and/or capsizing having just rounded the windward mark.
- Poor spinnaker gybes, resulting in twisted spinnakers.
- Broaching and/or capsizing around the leeward mark.

Most of the above problems arise during medium to strong winds, but some – especially poor spinnaker gybes resulting in a twisted spinnaker – also occur in lighter winds.

Now let's look in more detail at the problems of boat handling around marks and to try to eliminate the mistakes being made.

In the mid to upper wind range, it is important to raise the centreboard half way, and be ready to ease the mainsheet and hike out. Less rudder is now required to turn the boat and speed is maintained. Here is a good example.

Choppy seas need softer rig tension, giving maximum roundness and power into this jib to help the boat punch through the waves. In these conditions we are not so interested in pointing ability, as we are in speed over and through the waves. Full sails with leech twist is what is required in these conditions.

Rounding the windward mark – doublehanders

Often, in medium to strong winds, boats sail around the windward mark balanced to leeward with the rudder blades making that familiar gurgling sound. This means that the sails are not being used to turn the boat away from the wind, and as a result they will broach and may even capsize.

If you round the windward mark in medium to strong winds, in a doublehanded boat using the jib, using mainsail and bodyweight for balance, this stalling and broaching will not happen. You must go around the weather mark with the least amount of rudder movement by getting the boat in balance to steer itself. First of all, the boat balance must be kept upright and slightly to windward; as you bear away, initially the jib is kept in and eased more slowly than the mainsail, and at the same time the combined weight of the helmsman and crew must come aft along the gunwale to enable the lee-bow to lift off the water so that the bow will want to go off to leeward. The extent that the lee-bow lifts off the water depends on the type of boat that you sail. It is very effective in boats with deep 'V' sections forward of the mast and with large genoas, and also in boats with large mainsails and small jibs.

By combining the above points you will round the weather mark in balance with the least amount of rudder and pressure. If it's possible, it will also pay you to raise the board a little before you bear away, by luffing slightly as you get to the mark and raising the board with an efficient system.

Rounding the windward mark – singlehanders

Basically, the same applies to singlehanders as it does to doublehanders – except that it is very important to make any board adjustment before rounding the mark and, in the case of the Laser and Topper, making the necessary clew and kicking strap adjustments prior to the rounding – with the mainsail in and the boat balanced slightly to windward. Do not bring the board up too much, or you may capsize to windward having borne away.

Rounding the gybe mark – doublehanders

The main problem with this manoeuvre is the spinnaker handling and carrying out a controlled gybe. The important points to remember were described earlier.

Rounding the gybe mark – singlehanders

In a singlehander, as you bear away into the gybe you must ease the mainsail with the boat trimmed fairly well aft. At the same time as bearing away, look for the leech starting to move; and as it starts, go across the boat quickly to prevent the outboard end of the boom hitting the water on completion of the gybe. Also on completion of the gybe, be prepared to pull the mainsail in to prevent a possible capsize to windward. You have to be quick in a breeze – which brings us back to flexibility in the body, speed of reaction and fitness!

Rounding the leeward mark – doublehanders

The main problems that doublehanders experience when rounding the leeward mark are usually:

- Misjudging the speed of approach and taking the spinnaker down too late or too early.
- Taking the spinnaker (non-shute boats) down incorrectly – so that it is twisted the next time it goes up.
- Altering boat tuning controls too late.
- Balancing the boat to leeward, resulting in broaching.

The speed of approach to the leeward mark must be understood so that you are ready to round the leeward mark with the spinnaker stowed and the cunningham hole, kicking strap, clew outhaul and centreboard adjustments all made so that the boat is set up correctly for the next windward leg.

In stronger winds, the centreboard can be adjusted after rounding to reduce the risk of broaching during the rounding. In non-shute boats, the spinnaker must be taken down to windward, having got rid of the pole; the guy should be pulled until the tack of the spinnaker is in hand, then the helmsman releases the halyard, and the spinnaker is pulled down by the luff with the remainder on top. This will guarantee that the spinnaker will not go up twisted the next time it is used.

Another point that is sometimes forgotten is the tightening up of the spinnaker sheets (either by the helmsman or the crew) to prevent them from trailing astern.

Rounding the leeward mark – singlehanders

When rounding the leeward mark in a singlehanded boat, you should observe the following points:

- In the lighter wind range, adjustments to the daggerboard, cunningham hole,

Get your weight out and off the boat as soon as possible to prevent the boat from turning turtle. Here the crew must go into the water, around the transom, checking rudder on the way and then on to the centreboard with the helm. Or he must lie in the water where he is and be scooped in as the helm rights the boat, if physically strong enough.

kicking strap and clew outhaul should be made *prior* to the rounding.
- In medium to strong winds, these adjustments (apart from the cunningham hole) should be done *after* the rounding.

Having rounded the leeward mark correctly,

with the boat in balance (slightly pinched and balanced to windward in the case of a Laser and Topper), adjustments can be made to the kicking strap, clew and daggerboard. The tiller extension can be held between thumb and forefinger during these adjustments, or trapped under your backside! It is important that these adjustments are made on completion of rounding, and it will also help reduce the risk of you broaching and/or capsizing. You must get the daggerboard down after the rounding, as this will reduce the risk of broaching and capsizing before the rounding.

5

Boat Tuning

Boat tuning is rated highly in some training programmes based mainly on the following:

- **A** Type of boat
- **B** Course to be sailed
- **C** Expected sea conditions
- **D** Expected wind speeds

Golden rules of boat tuning:

1 *Do not get obsessed by it*   Remember that it is only one aspect of our sport. You could have the fastest boat on the water, but point it in the wrong direction or be unable to handle it correctly, or not know the rules, and it will count for nothing.

2 *Calibrate and record*   Everything must be marked and calibrated so that you can keep a good Boat Tuning Log (Appendix 1) and be able to refer to it after every race or boat tuning session.

3 *Do not forget the basics*
Flat water =   flatter sails, firmer leeches
Choppy water = fuller sails, more leech twist
Firmer leeches = more power/pointing ability
Leech twist =   more speed, less pointing

Hull finish

The outer hull must have a good finish and any slot gaskets and self bailers must be faired into the hull. A dull matt finish is normally preferred, as this results in a better water separation between the hull and the water; the same would apply to the foils. Check that the foils are in line while in the fully down position. To do this, turn the boat upside down (dinghies only!) and from fixed points measure that the foils are in alignment and that they are in the middle of the boat. In the past, some have been found to be slightly out, hence the reason for pointing higher on one tack than the other.

The following paragraphs cover more fully the aforementioned points **A–D**:

A The type of boat raced dictates the amount of time to be spent on this aspect of the sport. *Question*: Are you racing a speed machine, a tactical machine or both? **Speed machine** = Boats that go fast in straight lines and may tack very rarely for the windward mark, eg Tornado, Flying Dutchman. **Tactical machine** = Boats with speeds that are very close to each other, and therefore tactics come more into play, eg Enterprise, 470, 420, GP14, Laser, Topper.

People who race speed machines do tend to get much more involved in the subject of boat tuning as they are always looking for that extra edge in speed. Those who race more tactical boats generally prefer the 'If it looks good and feels good, get on with the race' attitude, only adjusting the controls for each point of sailing and changes in the sea/wind state.

B Course to be sailed   In some classes, championship courses can assist in the decision as to what type of rig to develop. For example, more upwind work than downwind work would necessitate more development of your fore-and-aft sails. More reaching than running would mean developing faster reaching spinnakers, etc. This area must be given some thought when developing sails for a particular championship.

C Expected sea conditions   You can assess what the sea conditions can be like at your venue by studying geographical data as well as local information. Therefore you should develop your sails for the expected conditions. Talk to your sailmakers and do not forget the basic theory that has already been mentioned.

D Expected wind speeds Expect anything! Do not be misled by predictions! Generally speaking, your rig must be flexible enough to cater for any wind speed. You must be able to both power up and down as required, within your class rules.

Boat tuning controls

The following boat tuning controls are available to the majority of yachts/dinghies, the theory of which is the same for every boat:

1 The mast	7 Kicking strap
2 Spreaders	8 Barber haulers
3 Rig tension	9 Spinnaker pole
4 Mast ram/	height
chocks/strutt	10 Centreboard
5 Cunningham hole	positions
6 Clew outhaul	11 Traveller/bridle

1 The mast

Have you got the best section for your all-up weight combination as allowed in your class rules? The heavier you are, the stiffer the section can be to keep maximum power in a higher wind speed.

Mast heel position: is this in the correct position? The best test for this is to sail the boat close-hauled in a force 2–3 breeze with flat water, let the tiller go, and the boat should *slowly* luff head-to-wind. If she luffs quickly, then the mast heel is too far aft. If she does not luff at all, or worse still bears away, then the heel is too far forward. While sailing close-hauled, the boat should have approximately 4° of weather helm.

Mast rake position: every class of boat has an optimum mast rake position for light, medium and strong winds, and also for flat or choppy water. Mast rake is normally measured in the following way: using the main halyard, pull up a long tape measure to the black band and measure to the top of the transom on the centreline. As an example, a 420 in light airs would be 6.1m (20ft 3in); in medium airs 6m (19ft 10in); and in strong winds, 5.9m (19ft 7in). Know your measurements for your class and use them every time.

2 Spreaders

Spreaders are a most critical boat tuning control. If allowed in your class rules, you must be prepared to adjust both the length and the angle of your spreaders to achieve the desired mainsail camber and leech shape for the conditions of the day. The theory is as follows:

Longer spreaders: make the mast stiffer sideways, giving more power and better pointing ability. This is most common in

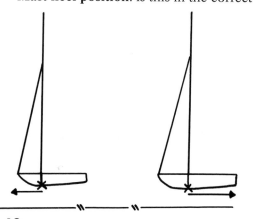

generally underpowered boats with high aspect ratio jibs and little overlap behind the mainsail. These spreaders always deflect the shrouds outboard from the straight line between the chainplate and the hounds; the amount depends on the class of boat and mast section being used. Compare yours with that of friends' boats of approximately the same weight and mast section.

Short spreaders: pull the shrouds inboard from the straight line. This allows the mast to be brought to windward at spreader height, thereby depowering the mainsail and allowing the top section to fall off to leeward, thus releasing the upper mainsail leech and allowing it to twist open more easily; this reduces the healing moment of the boat and increases speed. Be careful not to overdo it, thereby losing too much power and pointing ability. This setting is most common in generally overpowered boats with large overlapping genoas, eg Flying Dutchman or GP14 in the upper wind range.

Medium-length spreaders (shrouds in line with chainplate and hounds): here the mast is just supported and not induced to do anything by the spreaders. The mast will bend fore-and-aft plus sideways within its own characteristics. This is a common setting in Enterprises.

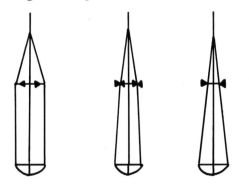

Spreader angle:
Forward: deflecting the shrouds forward restricts the mast from bending further forward, which is good for retaining mainsail

camber and power and holding the mainsail leech shape in the middle wind range and choppy water.
Middle (shrouds in line): here the mast will bend once again within its own characteristics forward and, to a degree, to windward.
Aft (deflecting shrouds aft): now we are trying to induce pre-bend, with the rig in tension trying to push the mast forward at this point, to flatten the mainsail more and further open the leech. This is very effective in boats with large mainsails, in the upper wind range, in order to depower and reduce the healing moment of the boat along with weather helm.

3 Rig tension
Theory: Flat water requires a tighter rig tension
Choppy water requires less rig tension

Tighter rigs offer more power and pointing on flat water. Softer rigs offer less power and pointing in choppy seas, but more speed as the boat pounds through the waves. Also, the boat doesn't break up so easily in these conditions – something must give and flex! How tight of slack the rig is obviously varies from class to class.

Compare with friends, and also have your rig tension meter handy for checking readings both before and after a race.

4 Mast ram/chocks/strutt
Although often overlooked, this control alone can be responsible for power and pointing ability. It is used in conjunction with the spreaders, clew outhaul, kicking strap and cunningham hole tensions to gain maximum power and pointing ability.

Pre-start spreader lengths and angles are altered for maximum speed and pointing ability as the conditions change. Know your rig and settings (Race Training Boat Tuning Serials).

Maximum power is being got out of this rig with a stiff mast sideways at spreader height and above, supporting the mainsail leech. There is good twist in the upper leech for speed through the waves, with power and pointing ability coming off the lower leech. The jib sheet lead is also good for power and pointing ability, with the slot area between jib leech and mainsail set to just lift the luff area of the mainsail below spreader height. If you felt underpowered and/or needed better pointing ability, close the mid-upper leech slightly by using a touch more mainsheet tension and/or kicker tension and/or a touch more mast ram on.

unga-Tallberg

Broaching with the rudder blade hard over and thus acting as a brake and slowing the boat down, because both the helm and crew are too far forward (digging in the lee-bow), with the kicking strap too tight, and the centreboard most probably too far down. The crew is not on her toes to give extra leverage outboard. Correct these points to prevent this occurring.

Ease the mast ram off to create a flatter mainsail and to produce a finer flatter entry into the mast low down in the slot area. This is very good when racing on flat water in any wind speed. This also allows the mainsail leech more readily to twist open, so be prepared to control the leech shape using the kicker, cunningham and clew outhaul controls (to be described later).

The more *mast ram on*, the straighter the mast becomes fore-and-aft, therefore giving you more power with more depth of camber in the mainsail, and subsequently a mainsail leech that wants to stand up and return to windward more readily. Powered-up mainsails are good in the light to medium wind range on choppy confused seas, but be

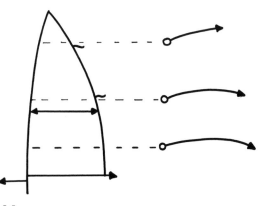

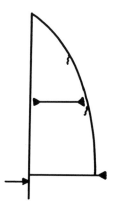

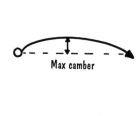

Max camber

Mast bend fore and aft low down is kept straight in these conditions to put maximum power and fullness back into the mainsail, thus giving maximum speed through the choppy sea. Once again there is less interest in pointing ability and more in speed.

very careful not to have a leech shape that is standing too firm, preventing the wind escaping off the leech. Watch your telltales, kicker and traveller positions (to be described later).

5 Cunningham hole

Horizontal creases coming away from the luff of the mainsail in the lower third area of the sail are often known as speed bumps! They are not detrimental to boat speed.

Draw a line down the sail approximately 45–55 per cent back from its leading edge; this is the maximum point of camber area built in by the sailmaker. As the wind increases across this aerofoil shape, the maximum point of camber is pushed back towards the leech area and makes the leech want to stand firm, therefore increasing the

heeling moment of the boat and weather helm, thus slowing you down. So to correct the problem, tension the cunningham hole to bring the centre of effort maximum point of camber back to where it is designed to be. This will allow the leech to open, and reduce the heeling moment and weather helm, enabling the boat to go faster through the

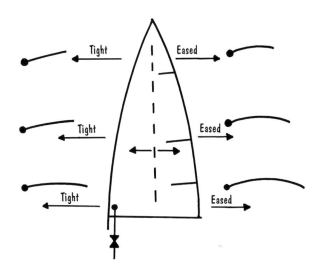

Whilst reaching, the cunningham hole is eased to put maximum power back into the mainsail and therefore allow the leech to stand. Only tension the cunningham if you are overpowered on a reach to help blade out the mainsail and open the leech, to allow the wind to escape off it and reduce the heeling moment of the boat as well as the weather helm.

water. The harder it blows, the tighter it needs to be while beating and reaching. On a run, always east it off across the wind range.

(*Note*: On flat water, at any wind speed, it has been proved that maximum tension gives the ability to go fast and point high – especially in singlehanders. Try it, even in light airs, and see what *your* conclusions are.)

6 Clew outhaul

Critical in its positioning, the clew outhaul control alone can be responsible for both speed and pointing ability. Basic guidelines are as follows: *Sailing to windward*: tensioned all the way out to the back band –

the only one possible exception to this being in the light to medium wind range on open sloppy, choppy seas, when you may require a deeper, more powerful, sail with less pointing ability. *Reaching and running*: tensioned all the way out to the black band for maximum projection area, controlling the leech shape by using kicker and cunningham controls. Only ease the clew outhaul on these points of sailing if, in your class of boat, the mainsail is relatively flat and open leeched and you wish to power it up more.

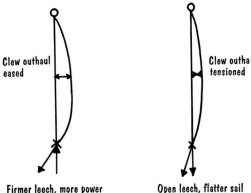

Clew outhaul eased — Firmer leech, more power

Clew outhaul tensioned — Open leech, flatter sail

Good lower slot shape, giving maximum power and pointing ability from the jib. It is also important, with a mainsail too deep in the window area, to keep the main clew outhaul fairly tight in order not to choke the slot shape, which would stall the wind passing around the leeward side of the mainsail and impair boat speed.

7 Kicking strap

This is probably the most important boat tuning control, overlooked by many racing people on each point of sailing. This control is responsible for the following: *boat speed, pointing ability and boat stability*. It affects the depth of the mainsail camber and the mainsail leech shape. Kicking strap tension to windward is used to achieve the correct mainsail leech shape for the conditions of the day, and while racing it is used in close conjunction with your mainsail leech telltales.

While sailing to windward the basic guidelines are as follows: your upper and middle telltales should be streaming 80 per cent of the time and stalling 20 per cent. This indicates to you that the leech shape is correct for the wind speed at the time. As wind speed increases and the boat becomes overpowered, you will now induce more leech twist and the telltales will stream all the time, thereby reducing the healing moment of the boat and weather helm. In classes where the distance between the mast and mainsail leech at the top batten area is quite small, eg J24, Soling or Dragon, you may have the top telltale stalling 80 per cent and streaming 20 per cent to achieve the correct leech shape while sailing to windward, in order to achieve good pointing ability.

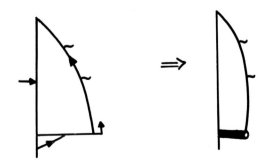

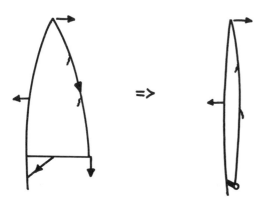

Perfection! However, to depower the mainsail they will need to tension the clew outhaul and cunningham and ease the kicking strap slightly.

Kicking strap tension while running: in light airs: kicker off to maintain twist and speed. In medium airs: kicker on, just enough for the top batten to hold up for power. In strong winds: kicker on tight to close upper leech and assist stability, reducing the risk of the death roll!

As you can see, the kicker has a great deal to answer for. Don't forget that as the kicker is tensioned in dinghies and small keel boats, the mast will bend – thereby creating a flatter mainsail, which is good for flat water, any wind speed.

The kicker tension on each point of sailing is critical, so ensure it is adjusted accordingly.

Kicking strap tension while reaching: again this should be just enough to achieve your 80 per cent streaming and 20 per cent stalling or, in the upper wind range, streaming all the time so that you are not overpowered. Do not forget, if overpowered on a reach, to ease the kicker to create more upper mainsail leech twist, less healing moment and less weather helm.

8 Barber haulers

This is a combination of lead blocks and track(s) to control the clew of a headsail. The positioning of the clew is critical, affecting both boat speed and pointing ability; therefore it is an important control to evaluate during boat tuning serials with a particular headsail. The positioning of the headsail lead block dramatically affects:

- depth of headsail camber
- leech shape

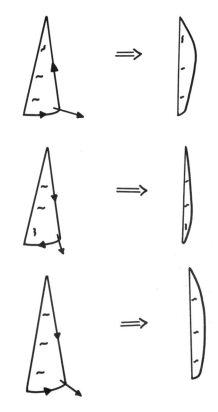

The further forward the lead block is taken, the deeper the camber becomes and the harder the leech. The further aft the lead block goes, the less camber there is, as the sail becomes flatter and has more leech twist – especially higher up. As you take the lead block further outboard (class rules permitting), you create a wider slot area between the headsail leech and the leeward side of the mainsail and narrow the slot shape as you progressively come further inboard.

General theory for positioning the barber haulers:

1 Sloppy/choppy open sea venues require fuller headsails with mid to upper leech twist, to achieve both power and speed.

2 Flat water venues require flatter headsails with firmer leeches to achieve maximum pointing ability. (*Caution*: Do not go *too flat*, especially with the luff area of the sail, as this will create too much loss of power.)

3 Light to medium winds – close the slot area to increase power and pointing.

4 Medium to strong winds – open the slot area progressively, as the boat becomes over-powered, to twist open the mid to upper leech, thereby reducing the heeling moment of the boat and weather helm to develop more speed.

Use of headsail telltales (in conjunction with the barber haulers): these should be spaced equally apart, approximately 15 cm (6 in) from the luff, and be about 10 cm (4 in) long. They should also be stuck clear of any seams and stitching. There should be one at mid height, one in the top third area, and one in the lower third area.

When racing, while beating and reaching all three telltales on the weather side should be streaming just above the horizontal, and those on the leeward side should be horizontal. If the top telltale streams too high, there is too much upper leech twist, so take the barber hauler or lead block further

The kicking strap is far too tight for these light airs, it should be completely slack, enabling the top and middle tell tales to stream off the leech, with the boom being kept on the centreline, going to windward. Here with this leech shape too much drag is being created as the wind tries to get off the leech, therefore killing boat speed.

For the middle wind range this 420 needs to get the boom more on the centreline and, more important, close the lower slot area by barber-hauling the jib. This will also give a more uniform slot shape with the jib leech, and better pointing ability.

forward. Conversely, if the lower telltale is stalling, the lower third area of the headsail is too deep – so take the lead slightly further aft until it streams correctly.

General guide: When racing to windward, the mainsail should just be beginning to lift. If it isn't, then the slot shape is too open. If it is lifting excessively, then the slot shape is too closed.

9 Spinnaker pole height

This control is critical for downwind speed and trimmer control. The spinnaker pole height at both ends is often overlooked. The guidelines are:

Reaching: (a) the spinnaker luff should always be trimmed so that it is on the

curl/full; (b) the initial curl should be at mid height. If higher, the pole is too low; if lower, then the pole is too high.

Running: (a) tack and clew should be the same height: (b) in strong winds do not let the clew go to windward of the forestay. If the class rules permit, try to have both the guy and sheet lead forward near the shrouds to reduce spinnaker oscillation across the bow of the boat, thereby assisting stability downwind. During heavier gusts, overtrim the spinnaker to hide part of it behind the mainsail.

10 Centreboard positions

To windward in light to medium airs: if it is allowed within your class rules, the leading edge of the board should be just forward of the vertical. As the boat becomes over-powered in stronger winds, it should be allowed to swing aft of the vertical to assist in decreasing weather helm.

Reaching: the centreboard should be in the halfway position, decreasing the profile as the boat becomes over-powered to assist

In flight, at maximum speed, note the upper jib leech twist to give speed off the leech and not stall the air between jib, leech and mainsail. Be careful, though, not to lose too much power out of the jib by undersheeting it.

boat balance and reduce weather helm. Similarly, increase the profile as the boat becomes depowered and/or suffers from lee helm.

Running: in light airs the centreboard should be all the way up, but be careful now not to capsize to windward.

In the mid to upper winds there should be just enough centreboard showing to enable you to stand on it when you capsize! That is, the halfway position.

11 Traveller/bridle

Theory: Traveller = Sea venues
        Bridle   = Flat water venues

Traveller: this has three basic positions:

- To windward for light airs, sloppy seas to induce leech twist, fullness and speed.

- Midships – to power up the leech for both pointing ability and speed.
- To leeward for more mast bend, to flatten the mainsail and create a firm leech. Good for depowering and pointing ability in stronger winds and flatter water.

Bridle: with the bridle system the mainsail leech shape is controlled primarily by the kicking strap, but you must now use

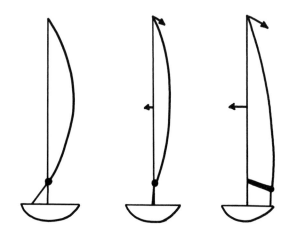

more mainsheet trimming to maintain boat balance – especially in the mid to upper wind range. In light airs with a slack kicking strap you cannot acquire enough mainsail leech twist unless your bridle system is on a carriage what can be brought up to the weather side of the boat.

Either the traveller or the bridle combined with the kicker and mainsheet tension are used in conjunction with your leech telltales as already discussed.

Deck control

Make sure that at deck level your mast is stiff sideways to ensure good control of the

mast sideways higher up. This will also improve your power and pointing ability, especially in all the boats with small overlapping higher aspect ratio jibs. Only those more over-canvased boats, with larger headsails and mainsails, would consider allowing the mast to move sideways at deck level as they become over-powered, thus allowing the mast to move to windward at deck level, mid-height level; and also to move to leeward at the top, helping to depower the mainsail and at the same time create a wider slot shape between jib leech and mainsail – thereby maintaining maximum straight line speed.

Conclusion

All the above-mentioned boat tuning controls and basic theory should be fully evaluated across all the wind/sea states, and therefore, if possible, should be included in your pre-event training.

6

Race Strategy

Visualise yourself in the starting of a championship course. The first leg of the course is a windward one, and the windward mark is 1.25 km away. The usual question asked by a competitor is, 'Which is the correct way to go?' The answer to this question depends on the following key factors:

- weather forecast
- surrounding land masses
- tide/surface current
- starting plan

Weather forecast

You must obtain the latest up-to-date weather forecast, including information on wind direction and strength. If the direction of the wind is forecasted to shift in either direction, your strategy plan must be to use and protect the appropriate side of the course right from the start. As the race progresses, changes in cloud formations must be looked for as these would indicate that there may be an imminent change in wind direction – for example, *cold frontal cloud*, early visual signs of a cold front arriving are low stratus clouds followed by active deepening cumulonimbus clouds associated with rain. As you look up to windward over the race area and see this lot approaching, you may well feel like saying, 'Time to go home!' But that, of course, would be the end of your race!

You will be seeing the wind increasing in velocity and, more important in the Northern Hemisphere, you will note that it is shifting left (backing). (In the Southern Hemisphere it would be veering clockwise.)

If and where possible, you should position yourself strategically on the port side of the course on port tack, being lifted up to the windward mark as the front approaches. Ensuring that you do not get too close to the port lay line, in this example, otherwise you will end up easing sheets to get to the windward mark having overstood it. As the leading edge of the front passes overhead it may well be raining, but you are still enjoying yourself because racing is FUN! Behind the front, the wind will decrease in velocity and veer, lifting you now on starboard tack up to the weather mark, where you will arrive as the sun shines – leading the fleet, of course, having used this information in the correct manner!

Following behind a cold front will be clearer skies, a blustery air stream and

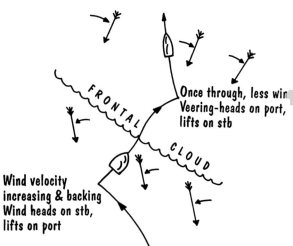

Once through, less win
Veering-heads on port,
lifts on stb

Wind velocity
increasing & backing
Wind heads on stb,
lifts on port

Whilst in the starting area you will have already decided on your race strategy from knowledge already gained both ashore and by sailing the beat earlier. From this knowledge you will also know your approximate position on the starting line so that you can go the way you want to go and not be forced off in the opposite direction.

higher cumulus clouds. Under the cumulus clouds there will be less wind as the air is rising underneath them, whereas in the clear blue sky area there will be more wind, which will normally lift you on to starboard tack in the gusts. (*Cumulus clouds*: these are fair weather clouds associated with high pressure.)

While you are in the area of the leeward mark, look up to windward: if there are more clouds over the port side of the course, go right of middle up the beat, because there will be more wind in the clear blue sky area. And vice versa if there is more cloud on the starboard side of the course.

Summary: Avoid sailing under cumulus clouds as there is less wind underneath them.

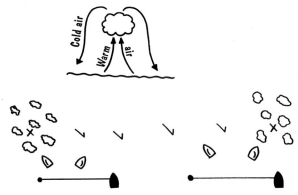

Gusts

When racing in gusty conditions behind a cold front, the tactician of the boat must be looking for the gusts on the water and calling them to the helmsman. (Singlehanders are on their own for this one, I'm afraid!) This is not only so that the helm is ready to react to the gust in feathering and depowering, but also to check whether or not you think that it is a lift or a heading gust. If it is a lifting gust, you stay on course;

if it is a header, you must consider tacking (if this action seems the correct tactical decision to make at this time, taking into consideration the other boats around you). If the centre of the gust is broad on your weather bow, it will lift you; if fine, it will head you; if slightly to leeward and ahead, be ready to capsize to windward!

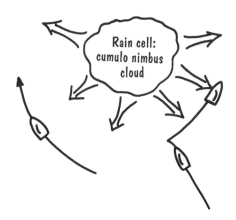

Surrounding land masses

Prior to a race at a venue, you must survey any surrounding land masses close to the race area. This can be achieved before getting to a race venue by studying a local chart. With the weather forecast in mind, look aloft at the clouds, if there are any, to establish the gradient wind direction. In the Northern Hemisphere the wind over the water is backed in relation to the gradient wind by 10–15°. Over the land, where there is greater friction, it can be 30–35°. (In the Southern Hemisphere it is veered by the same amounts.) Keeping these key figures in mind, the following golden rules apply in race strategy.

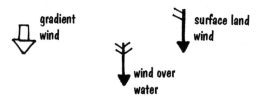

Converging wind produces more wind on the port side, so go left. Also, as the wind tries to leave the shore at right angles, you will be headed as you approach the land on starboard tack and lifted on port tack, so *do not get to the port lay line too early*.

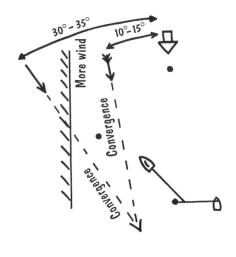

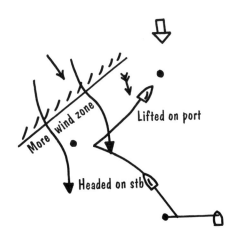

With an offshore wind you will have an oscillating breeze. Key points to remember are: the closer to the shore you go, the greater the oscillations from max left to max right (maybe as much as 60°; and also, the more frequent they become within one to two minutes. The further offshore you go, the less frequent they become (two to five minutes) and over a narrower arc (0–20°).

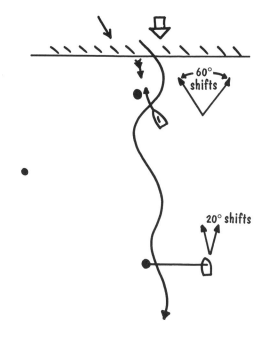

In the Northern Hemisphere, the first shear of the wind leaving the land is to the right, so approximately half a mile offshore you can expect to be lifted on starboard tack as you approach the windward mark. As you then progress closer inshore, expect to be headed on starboard and lifted on port. This effect happens off any coastline. The distance to seaward depends upon:

- wind speed
- height of land – the higher the land, the further to seaward the wind shear will be

In this scenario, wind shift tracking is essential to establish which is going to be the lifting tack at start time out of the start line in order that we are in sequence with the wind shifts as we progress up the beat. Also, do not get to either the port or starboard lay lines too early; if you do, you may find yourself easing sheets to get to the windward mark. Best to use the wind shifts up the middle of the course – be conservative. Remember that whilst standing on a weather shore looking down wind there is more wind at sea than you realise. With the land

mass lying at a tangent on the starboard side of the course, you now have a Catch 22 situation with regard to the quickest way up the beat:

- With the diverging land and sea arrows, there is less wind on the starboard side of the course.
- If the land is relatively high, there will be a header on port tack with a lift on starboard tack as the wind tries to leave the shoreline at right angles.

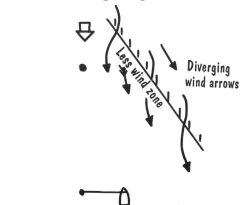

If the land is low this effect is minimal. In this situation it normally pays to be more in the middle/left of the course for more wind, unless you have a definite shift inshore, without losing too much velocity.

With the land mass now running parallel to the race area on your starboard side, go left of middle up the beat as there will be

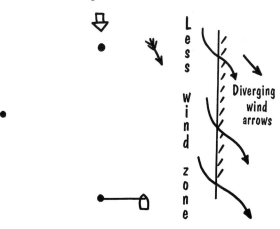

more wind. With diverging land and water arrows, there is less wind on the starboard side nearer the shore. Also, as you go in on port tack you will tend to be lifted on port tack as the wind off the water tries to cross on to the land at right angles.

With an onshore wind you now have your most stable wind in both direction and velocity (assuming that you are not expecting either a warm or cold front to come through, and that this is not a sea breeze).

Wind most stable
in direction & velocity
across the race area

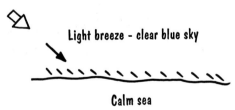

The key point to remember with an onshore wind is that there is less wind at sea than you realise while standing on a lee shore.

Sea breezes

If no gradient wind is present on a morning with a clear blue sky, then this is an early sign for a good sea breeze day, especially if early in the morning there is a light offshore

Light breeze - clear blue sky

Calm sea

wind indicating that there has been a night land breeze. At approximately 1100 hours, cumulus clouds will start to form over land with no cloud to seaward.

This indicates that warm air is rising above the land vertically; and as it cools, the clouds develop. As the warm air rises, cooler air above the water is drawn in off the sea to replace it. Thus the circulation of the sea breeze commences.

Initially you will get a local onshore breeze with no wind further to seaward, but as the circulation is completed, approximately 1200–1300 hours, a good sea breeze will fill in from the sea, up to force 4–5. Sea breezes tend to fill in just left of the right angle, ie from 340° on a north coast, 070° on an east coast, 160° on a south coast, and 250° on a west coast. They then stabilise with strength, approximately 20–30° to the right. Later on in the day (1500 hours plus), the sea breeze on all coasts tends to veer and decrease. So always go to the starboard side of the course as the race progresses in order to get the expected veer.

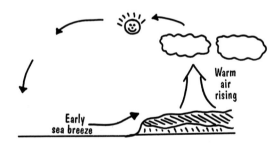

Early
sea breeze

Warm
air
rising

Sea breeze and gradient winds

If a strong gradient wind is present, a sea breeze cannot develop, although locally it can affect the velocity of the gradient wind. If a weak gradient wind is present (less than 20 knots), then a sea breeze can take over, but only as a weak one, for the gradient wind will oppose either the sea breeze circulation aloft or at sea level.

You may be going fast but is it in the right direction?

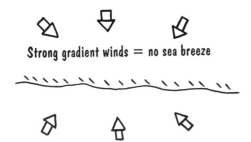

Strong gradient winds = no sea breeze

The basic guidelines are as follows:

If the gradient wind stays
at this angle there will not
be a sea breeze

A good sea breeze can develop if the gradient wind collapses early in the day. The sea breeze will come from a more veered direction perhaps later in the afternoon.

There will be a poor sea breeze, if at all, unless the gradient wind falls below 20 knots, allowing a sea breeze circulation to develop.

There will be a poor sea breeze, if at all, again depending on the gradient wind speed decreasing and the time of day. You could have a light breeze more backed to seaward and more veered closer to the shore.

There will be a poor sea breeze, if at all, if the gradient wind speed is 15–20 knots plus.

Tide/surface current

All the theory about wind and land, weather fronts and clouds can be turned inside out by the effect of tide or surface current on the day of the race. Every sea, large lake or reservoir has movement, and this has got to be detected and established before the start time of any important race. Charts, tidal atlases, local knowledge, tide sticks, prevailing wind directions, depths of water, changes in temperature of the water, and flat or choppy water across the course, all have to be considered in establishing water directional flow and strength. You must know what the tide/current is doing across the whole of the race area throughout the race period; all this is part of your race/championship preparation.

The following information is required to establish the following key points:

- Race strategy: which way to go?
- Starting plan.
- Lay line calls: beat/reach/run.

Race strategy

The starboard side of the course is favoured for the tide/current on the beat. Stay above rhumb lines for the reaches.

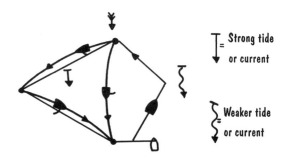

Strong tide or current

Weaker tide or current

The port side is favoured for the beat; stay low on the reaches. The starboard side is

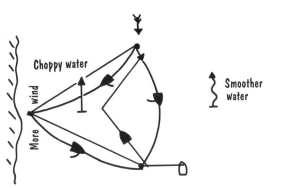

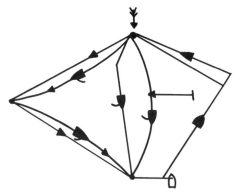

favoured for the run. Which is favoured for the wind? Catch 22!

Lee-bow as much as you can. Be above or on the port lay line for the windward mark, above the rhumb line for the first reach, and below on the second reach. Go for the starboard tack on the run, or port tack first, then back on to starboard for a faster point of sailing and better apparent wind.

reach, on it for the second reach, and go on starboard tack for the running leg or a short port tack then a long starboard. (It will be vice versa if the tide/current is the same angle from the right.)

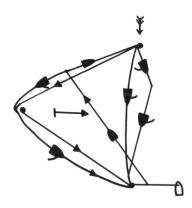

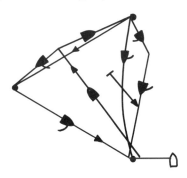

Going left up the beat will give you a shorter port lay line to judge into the mark, tacking just below it. For the first reach you will stay on the rhumb line, and on the second get below it when you can. For the

Again, lee-bow as much as you can. Sail above on the starboard lay line, low on the first reach, and high on the second. Gybe to start the run on a port tack or shortly after starting the run for better apparent wind and boat speed.

Go left up the beat and make your final approach above the port lay line. If you can lee-bow the tide or current, then even better – even if you do have to pinch slightly to do it.

Sail above the rhumb line for the first

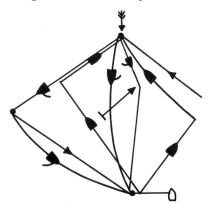

run, make a long starboard tack with better apparent wind (vice versa when tide is same angle from the right).

Starting plan

With the tide pushing people away from the line, look for opportunities to make a good port tack start or a late entry one at the starboard end. Or, with a good transit, a good start out of the middle.

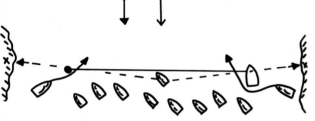

General recall time! Get the best out of the ends. When the one-minute or five-minute disqualification rule comes in, get a good start out of the middle if there is a good transit. Otherwise, stay at one end or the other, depending on which is the favoured side of the beat.

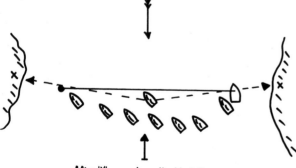

After 'X' general recalls, black flag rule will create a big sag to leeward grab your chance to be a star!

Use the tide and Rule 37.1 to cram the starboard end of the line with more freedom in the port half or quarter of the line.

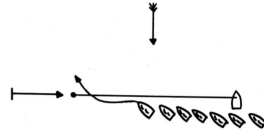

Use the tide/current to overcrowd and jam up the port end. A late entry could be made at the starboard end if this is the favoured end and/or you wish to go right up the beat.

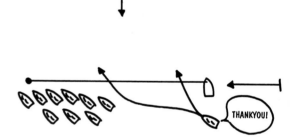

THANKYOU!

Race strategy is a fairly complex subject. However, as long as you take the time to study the theory and then apply it, together with your good boat speed and your ability to point in the right direction, then you should be among the chocolates at the end of the race! To quote a well-used phrase, 'It does not really matter where you are at the start of a race, what matters is where you are at the finish'!

7

Starting

You have planned, trained, and prepared both yourself and your boat, so now comes the crunch! The adrenalin is flowing, and you are about to start the race. The start is very critical. Although I maintain that a race is never lost until it is finished, the better the start, the more confidently you will sail the race, so read on.

The following are all significant factors in making a good start in every race:

Determination – controlled internal aggression
Concentration – must be at its maximum;
Anxiety level – must be controlled

Starting plan – related to line bias, tide or surface current and race strategy
Rules – in particular, *The Definition of Starting*: Rules 36, 37, 40, 41, 42 and 43
Transits – if possible
Sailing Instructions – knowledge of starting procedures, ie flags, one-minute and five-minute rules (if applicable), recall procedures, both individual and general.

The start: determination, concentration, controlled aggression, boat handling skills all put you in the right place at the right time. If they can do it, so can you. If you cannot, you need Race Training starting practise. Practise makes perfect.

In a race with a fleet of around 100 boats with the first mark approximately 0.75 m up the first beat on the open sea with an onshore wind that is stable in both velocity and direction, the start could be as much as 90 per cent of doing well. However, in contrast, in a round-the-world yacht race the start is of much less importance, only around 10 per cent, as long as you rank as a contender and start in accordance with the Sailing Instructions and the definition of starting.

Determination

What many people lack in their starting technique and ability is determination.

Off the line – maximum concentration on both boat speed and pointing ability is required to gain the edge over competitors on either side of you. In most classes this is essential for the first 100 metres off the line until you get the break, then you can change from the pointing mode to the speed mode, especially in choppy conditions.

Determination to be in the right place at the right time – that is what starting is all about. If you are in the wrong place, ie wallowing behind the line in other people's dirty wind, you will have made things much harder for yourself in that you will then have to get to the front of the fleet, relying on your boat speed, race strategy, good fortune or the others making mistakes. Determination should include 'internal aggression', which will make you determined to be in the right place at the right time. To coin a phrase, this is 'killer instinct'. However, this is an aggression that *must* be controlled – otherwise you may find yourself with a damaged boat and also in the protest room for infringement of the rules, with possible disqualification.

Anxiety level

In any race, the highest level of anxiety occurs during the pre-start period and at start time (except perhaps at the gybe mark in a force 6!). Learning to control this

anxiety comes with age and experience, and eventually you will become cooler and calmer at start times. For the benefit of the younger sailors and also newcomers to the sport, I include a few suggestions on how to bring this anxiety level down. First, try to relax mentally after the ten-minute gun by rehearsing your start in your head while standing up in the boat and breathing deeply. Always be alert for any changes in the conditions out on the race area.

Concentration

In the starting area in particular, your concentration level must be at its highest. You are in an area of water where there are many boats, all of which are trying to gain the same position as yourself, ie the best! You must therefore keep your eyes open and your wits about you the whole time.

The following are all key points on which to concentrate at this stage of the race:

- **Time/distance** – eg allow for tide or current, etc
- **Rules** – eg watch for lee-bow situations or boats trying to roll over the top of you
- **Positioning** – eg not being in dirty wind or to leeward in light winds, etc

Starting plan

Line bias: To establish the line bias for the start of the race, I suggest you use one of the following methods:

Method 1: Place the boat in the middle of the starting line area and then put her head-to-wind. Look either side of the beam to establish which end of the line (if any) is actually forward of the beam. If one end is, then that is the favoured end of the line from which to start.

This method is quite accurate and can be used on relatively short starting lines in small fleets. However, it is not recommended for long lines and large fleets.

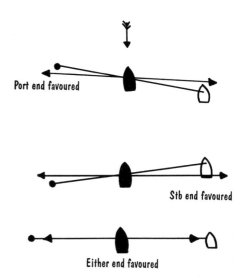

Port end favoured

Stb end favoured

Either end favoured

Method 2: This is a more accurate method to use. With the mainsail trimmed correctly, reach along the starting line, then tack – without moving the position of the mainsheet – and sail the reciprocal course along the line.

If the mainsail is luffing, or worse still flapping, you are sailing towards the correct end of the line from which to start. However, if after you have tacked and are sailing the reciprocal course the mainsail is overtrimmed and you have to east it, you are sailing away from the correct end from which to start.

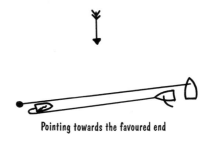

Pointing towards the favoured end

Method 3: The most accurate method is to use your compass. In this example I have first of all taken the starting line bearing 090°. From there you proceed into the

87

middle of the starting line and take a wind reading; in this example, with the boat head-to-wind, the reading is 000°. This tells you that you have a square starting line to the wind direction as it is at a right angle to the wind direction, and so either end of the line is favoured. However, if your wind reading was 010°, then the starboard end would be favoured by 10° as it is 10° closer to the wind direction; and alternatively if the wind direction was 350°, the port end would be favoured by 10°.

Chaos Corner! I'm afraid it does occasionally happen. Your main thoughts going into this mess should be: sail around it, delay gybing and go low on the next reach, especially if it is going to be a broad one. If the next reach is going to be tight, slow down and wait for a gap to develop as the raft goes round in a heap and low. You can gain many places here.
Rules – if there is contact and you are in the right make sure you get the number of the boat that hits you ready for the protest form. If you are in the wrong, take your penalty: on points at the end of an event it will make a difference.

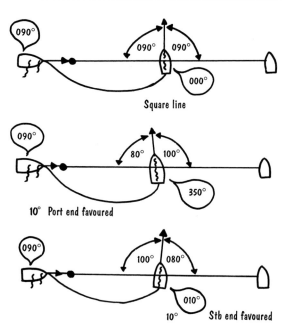

Square line

10° Port end favoured

10° Stb end favoured

Method 4: This method requires the compass and also establishing the tacking angle of the boat on the day of the race. To do this you pre-start tune your boat, check your compass heading close-hauled, tack,

and check your heading close-hauled on the *new* tack. That is your tacking angle.

From this angle you can establish the wind direction – it is half-way between the two closed-hauled compass headings. To see which is the favoured end of the line, first take the line bearing (again in my example it is 090° – from the port end), round the outer distance mark close-hauled on port tack, and then check the compass heading: it is 045°. If your tacking angle for the day is 90°, then you know that you must be sailing 45° off the wind direction, and so the wind reading in this example is 000°, giving you once again a square line to the wind. If, however, your close-hauled course was 055°, the wind would be 010°, making the starboard end favoured by 10° or, if your close-hauled course was 035°, the port end would be favoured by 10°.

Remember to check your line bearing after the five-minute gun, as up to that time the CRO can alter the line – and many of us have been caught out by this one in the past!

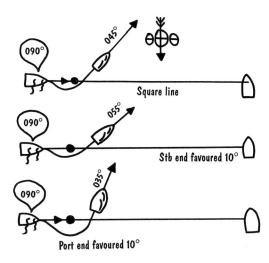

Having made a bad start, not a lot is lost by taking transoms on port tack as you get squirts of wind lifting you on port tack, keeping you in contact with the fleet. Next comes the header on port tack, you are lifted up on starboard tack and arrive at the windward mark in the top 3! It has been seen before!

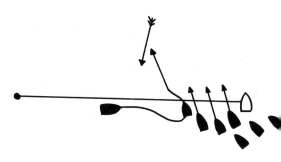

Once you have established which is the favoured end of the line (if any), you must now consider where on the line you need to position yourself at start time in relation to your race strategy. Remember the following key points:

- If you want to go left up the beat, start at the port end.
- If you want to go right up the beat, start at the starboard end.
- If you want to use the shifts up the middle, start in the middle – but only if you can obtain a good shoreline transit on the line and get on to the freeing tack at start time as soon as possible in order to be in sequence with the wind shifts.

Start in this area if wanting to go left	Start in this area if you want to work the shifts more up the middle and can get a transit	Start in this area if you want to go right

- If you wish to go right up the beat and the port end is favoured, start to windward of the bunch at the port end in a position where you can quickly tack on to port and go right.

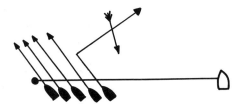

- If you wish to go left up the beat and the starboard end is favoured, always make a port tack approach along the line and tack below the bunch at the starboard end in a position to drive off to the port side of the course.

Rules

The rules in the starting area will be covered later in a more detailed section on the Racing Rules. However, in the meantime, the important rules to remember are these: The Definition of Starting (Part 1 of the Racing Rules), 36, 37, 40, 41, 42 and 43. These should be revised and memorised. You should also know the Sailing Instructions and recalls (Rule 8) and the one-minute rule Flag I (Rule 51.1(c)).

Transits

To gain a good start in land-locked areas it is essential, wherever possible, to establish a transit of the line. This is especially important if you wish to make a good start out of the middle of the line in shifty conditions. If you cannot find a good transit, do not start in the middle because you will find yourself either over the line or well behind it at start time. Once you have a transit, be confident about it and use it – especially in conditions where there is a tide pushing people away from the line and where the five- or one-minute disqualification rule is in force (as it is on these occasions when fleets are generally very 'line shy'). Therefore by using your transits you could get a cracking start and lead the fleet away from the line. Do remember to confirm your transit(s) after the five-minute gun to ensure that the line has not been altered by the CRO.

Gate start

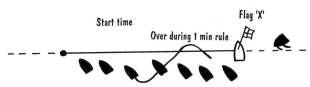

In the case of a gate start you are presented with a different proposition (refer to Gate Starting Procedures in the RYA Standard Sailing Instructions). The basic questions everyone asks are: when is the best time, and where is the best place to start? To answer these questions the following points must be considered:

- Am I faster than the 'pathfinder'?
- Which side of the beat do I want to be for the wind and the tide?
- Or do I want to work the shifts up the middle?
- Are we on a freeing tack out of the gate, or a heading tack?

Once you have thought about these points you will feel more confident about when to go. Other points to consider are boats to leeward and the occasional 'cowboy' trying to pass between yourself and the gate or the guard boat when there is no room for him! Finally, do not get to weather of the 'pathfinder' and find yourself having to run back to get round the guard launch or beyond the limit of the gate when it closes.

Sailing Instructions

The Sailing Instructions that specifically apply to starting procedure, recalls and penalties must be fully understood. Many competitors fall foul of either the one-minute rule or the five- or one-minute disqualification rule.

The one-minute 'round-the-ends' rule is indicated by Flag I hoisted with the preparatory signal. This means: 'Where any part of a yacht's hull, crew or equipment is on the course side of the starting line *or it's extensions* during the one-minute prior to the starting signal, it shall sail to the pre-start side of the line across one of its extensions and start.'

The Sailing Instructions may also indicate either a five- or one-minute disqualification rule indicated either by Pennant Numeral 9 or a black flag. Any boat entering the penalty area (ie that area within the windward mark and the port and starboard ends of the line) during the designated period will be disqualified from that race – or any subsequent starts of that race if the race is later abandoned or if there is a general recall. This area may also be defined by the start line and the leeward mark; it varies from event to event, so check your Sailing Instructions.

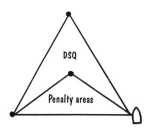

Be prepared, once the black flag rule has been introduced, to make a good start from either end of the line, or obtain a good transit and gain a good start from the middle, as on these occasions many of the competitors will definitely be 'line shy'.

In conclusion, starting is one aspect of the sport that some people excel at, but others never seem to master. However, practice makes perfect, and of course there are the other ten aspects with which to win the race. Your objective is to be a good all-rounder in the sport.

START – CONSOLIDATE – WIN

8

Tactics

The Golden Rules of tactics are:

1 **Start**
2 **Consolidate**
3 **Win**

If you combine this psychological approach with boat speed and race strategy, you should in a relatively short time become the best tactician in the fleet.

As a tactician in today's one-design racing you must have a sound knowledge of tactical manoeuvres in the following areas:

- Starting
- Windward legs
- Reaching legs
- Running legs

Tactics will always be related to both race strategy and the Racing Rules, and also to the following situations:

- Boat to boat
- Boat to group of boats
- Boat to fleet

Other key points to remember are:

1 When on the beat, you should always, generally speaking, take the tack that is taking you closest to the windward mark, especially in an oscillating breeze and shifty conditions as in landlocked areas or open sea venues with an offshore wind. There are exceptions to this basic tactical rule, but only for race strategy reasons such as tide/surface current, geographical wind bends or an expected wind direction change.

2 Stay between the majority of the fleet and the next mark in order to protect your position – *even* if you believe that they are going the wrong way. This is because you could lose out at the very end of the race if you sail your own course, but in the meantime a fluke occurs that enables those who went the 'wrong way' to come out best! Be conservative and consolidate what you have rather than risk your position by letting your opposition off the hook. The only exception to this theory is when you are in that very rare position known as DTP (down the pan!). At this point, you have nothing to lose, but a great deal to gain. Obviously, you will gain nothing by simply following the fleet around the course, and there is always a slim chance that you could get a lucky fluke if you go in the opposite direction!

Tactics in the starting area

These must be connected to your overall race strategy in as much as they depend on which direction you have decided to go up the first beat. *If you have decided to go left, up the first beat* then the tactics you must apply are as follows: start from the port end of the line if the port end is the favoured end from which to start; if not, start from the starboard end of the line, *but* to leeward of the group of boats at the starboard end.

If you have decided to go right up the first beat, then the tactics you must apply are as follows: start from the port end of the line, if that is the favoured end, *but* to weather of the group of boats at the port end. This will give you the chance to break out on to port tack early, and cross to the right-hand side of the course. However, if the starboard end of the line is favoured, you must be right up at that end – sometimes getting there early in order to guarantee your position.

If you wish to go up the middle of the first beat, start out of the middle area of the start line, but *only* if you can establish a good transit to enable you to make a good start without being too far behind the line or (perish the thought!) over the line at start time. If you cannot establish a good transit, do *not* start in the middle area; go to either end – obviously the favoured end if there is one, and/or the end of the line that will allow you to go the favoured way up the first beat.

Once you have decided where you want to be on the starting line, you must now address the question of how you are going to get there. Remember, you will only achieve your objective by using: determination, controlled aggression and concentration.

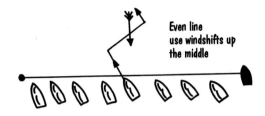

Even line
use windshifts up
the middle

Many top sailors will consider making a port tack approach to the starting line, therefore keeping their options more open.

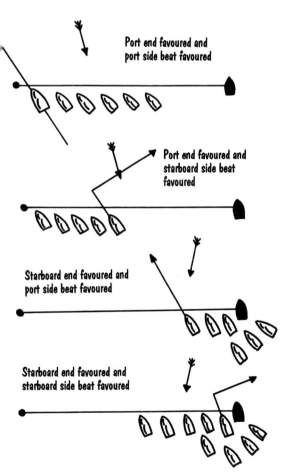

Port end favoured and port side beat favoured

Port end favoured and starboard side beat favoured

Starboard end favoured and port side beat favoured

Starboard end favoured and starboard side beat favoured

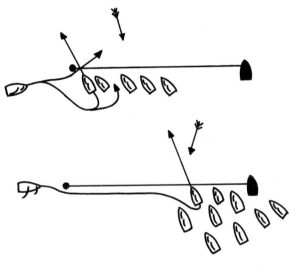

By approaching the line in this way, you get a much clearer view of how the start is developing, and you will encounter less hassle from other boats and from the rules.

Tactics on the beat

Having started, cleared the starting line (*in clear wind*) and progressed to your preferred area of the windward leg – left, middle or

93

right – the tactician must now begin to assess how the boat is positioned in relation to the rest of the fleet. Key points at this stage are:

A Are you going with the majority of the fleet? If not, why not?

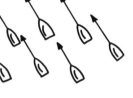

Are *you* using the correct race strategy theory or are *they*?

B Do you stay on this tack or go across and join the rest of the fleet?

C Are you on a lift or a header at the moment? If you are on a lift, stay on course; if you are on a header, perhaps you should tack.

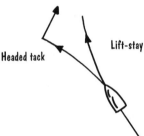

D How are you doing in relation to the rest of the fleet? Are you between the majority and the windward mark?

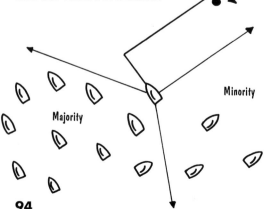

E Are you on the tack taking you closest to the windward mark?

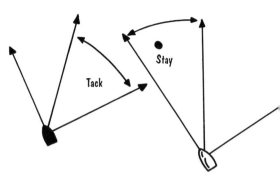

F Are you clear to tack if you need to?

All these questions should be going through a tactician's mind at this stage of the race, and all relevant information should be passed on to the helm in order that they can concentrate on sailing the boat fast and not be required to search around for this information themselves. However, be careful not to give them too much information at once, because too much information can be as bad as too little.

Points to consider on the windward leg: If you wish to cross the race area because of either a persistent wind shift, or to consolidate your present position and gain on the opposite side of the beat, then always try to cross the windward leg of the course in the middle where there will be fewer boats and less confused wind and water.

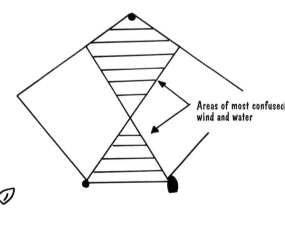

Situations on the windward legs

1 Tack for clear air and stay on port tack if port is lifting or if the starboard side is favoured. Or clear your air and come back on the starboard side if you are laying the mark or are on the tack taking you closest to it. Or, bear away at speed for clear air to leeward, if you are on the lifting tack or are laying the next mark with a long way to go to it.

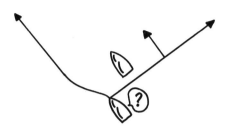

2 Tack below if you can lay the mark (marks to port), or if the tide/current is taking you from left to right and you are just below the lay line, or if you favour the port side of the course for either a favoured tide/current or an expectant backing wind shift. Bear away and take the opposition's transom for all other options.

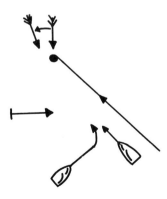

3 Sail the opposition on to guarantee your position, whether you are leaving the mark to port or starboard. This also applies if you are on port tack on the starboard lay line.

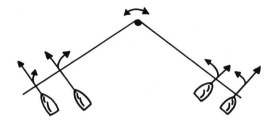

4 Call for water to tack, under Rule 43, to gain the advantage and a place. If you do not, and you bear away, you will have to give room to the boat on your weather quarter to clear the starboard tack obstruction as well. You will therefore lose the opportunity of gaining a place.

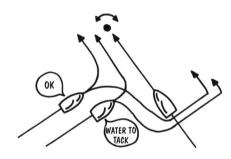

5 While high on a group of boats to leeward and in a lifting wind shift, go for speed and not for height – especially if you are next expecting a header with a backing shift. This works well in high-performance planing dinghies, but not in heavier displacement boats.

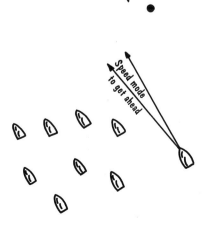

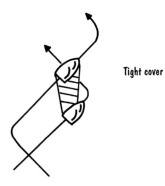

Tight cover

Loose cover: you would put a loose cover on an opponent if you wished to encourage them to continue on their present course because you believe it to be the correct way to go up the beat with the majority of the fleet.

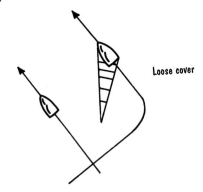

Loose cover

6 Tight cover or loose cover – boat to boat or boat to group covering situations are always occurring, and you must be prepared to take the appropriate action. *Tight cover*: You would place a tight cover on an opponent if you wished to: (a) slow them down, or (b) force them to tack off.

In this situation if starboard tack is favoured and/or a boat wishes to go to the left up the beat. ESP will have to drive off low initially and go for speed and clear air before coming back up again. Alternatively she will have to tack off for clear air as she will not live very long in this position.

There will also be times when you will wish to do a dummy tack to trap your opponent and force them to tack; this will once again slow them down by making them do a double tack. Likewise, as the attacking boat from behind, you can also throw in a dummy tack in order to try to break cover.

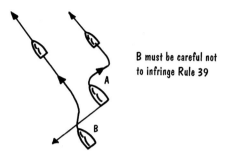

B must be careful not
to infringe Rule 39

You should not be on the lay line, far from the mark, with boats coming in and tacking on you, ahead of you or under your lee-bow.

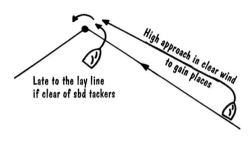

High approach in clear wind to gain places

Late to the lay line
if clear of sbd tackers

7 One of the most common mistakes made by tacticians is getting to the lay line early (port or starboard) when they are not in the leading group. Your options are as follows: (*a*) get there rather late and near the apex of the beat, or (*b*) get there early, but high to avoid the need to keep tacking off.

In the Northern Hemisphere, whilst racing in a blustery/gusty west to north west air stream, never go low on a reach as those to weather of you will pick up the gusts first and eventually roll over the top of you, as has happened here to the Australians.

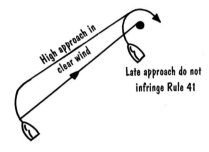

High approach in
clear wind

Late approach do not
infringe Rule 41

8 In this diagram, the boat on starboard tack can slow down and force the port-tack

boat to do one of two things: (*a*) take his stern and therefore not make the mark, or (*b*) tack off for the starboard tack boat, giving him more of a lead.

S slows - P must keep clear. S can then tack round, unless P just slows too!

These are just a few of the most common situations in which you are likely to find yourself while sailing the windward leg. Always try to keep calm, think positively about your next move(s) (rather like a chess player), and keep clear wind at all times. Also, never forget your basic race strategy before executing your moves.

Tactics on the reaching legs

No matter how long you try to put it off, you will eventually arrive at the windward mark where you will see the green filter arrow inviting you to turn either left or right and head for the gybe mark. The following are checks you should make during your final approach on the starboard lay line before rounding the windward mark (leaving it to port):

1 Check your compass course for the reaching legs. This should be 135° from the windward leg (assuming that the gybe mark is set with a 90° angle).

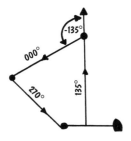

2 Check whether the wind direction is relatively stable or whether it is steadily backing in accordance with the weather forecast. If it is backing first go high down the reaching leg above your compass bearing. If the wind is veering and expected to go right, go low below your compass bearing.

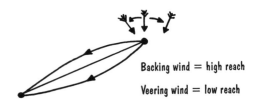

Backing wind = high reach

Veering wind = low reach

3 Check what the tide or surface current is doing and be ready to allow for it while pounding down the reaching leg.

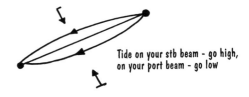

Tide on your stb beam - go high, on your port beam - go low

Having noted these key points and keeping them in mind throughout this leg of the course, there are now two more important factors that should be foremost in your mind:

• clear wind
• speed

Clear wind

As on any leg of the course, you must keep clear wind. The worst situation to be in is when you know that, for either wind or tidal reasons, the fastest way to go down the reach is below the rhumb line; but you also know that immediately behind you is a bunch of boats that, as soon as you go low, will sail over the top of you – taking your wind like one mass blanket. In this situation

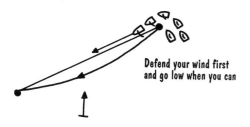

Defend your wind first
and go low when you can

you must protect your wind first and stay between the opposition and the next mark.

You will only have the freedom to sail your preferred course downwind when there is a significant gap between yourself and a group clear astern. This is equally true when reaching in gusty conditions. Never go low and allow the opposition to get high, catching the gusts before you and subsequently rolling over the top of you.

Speed

A successful fast reaching leg depends on all the following: **boat balance, boat trim, sail trim, gusts, lulls, waves** and **Rule 54**. In other words, *total concentration*! Never forget that sail leech twist generates speed in spinnakers, jibs and mainsails. On a reaching leg, too much twist loses power and increases instability, resulting in a capsize or broaching to windward. Closed leeches will reduce speed and also increase instability, again possibly resulting in a capsize or broaching to leeward. Therefore, you must have the correct amount of leech twist for both the sea state and wind speed at the time to maintain both stability and speed. Combine the above points with gusts and lulls. Bear away in the gusts and come

up in the lulls; likewise with the waves – bear away down the face and luff up before you hit the back. You will then have good speed down a reaching leg.

In one-design racing, because boat speeds are fairly equal, reaching legs tend to become a procession. Also, when sailing close together, and always defending their wind, the fleet tends to get relatively high on the rhumb line. Therefore the chances of you sailing over someone are relatively slim because they will most certainly be ready to defend themselves using both Rules 37 and 39. However, there is always the chance that they may make a mistake. A boat in the middle or the back of the fleet will see this happening ahead of them and can use this to their advantage by staying low and gaining towards the end of the reaching leg.

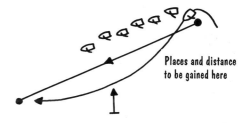

Places and distance
to be gained here

Towards the end of the leg, and as you approach the gybe mark, look around you and see how you are positioned in relation to the other boats and the Racing Rules. The rules that could apply as you approach and round are Rules 37, 39, 42 and 45.

The following scenarios are quite common at the gybe mark and require some forward thinking to establish a 'plan of action' should you find yourself in any of these situations:

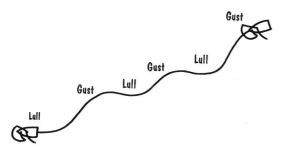

When clear to do so, always make your final approach to the gybe mark high to ensure a perfect rounding with the least amount of use of the rudder to maintain maximum speed throughout the rounding manoeuvre.

Crash gybe and out high for the second reach in clear wind, especially if this is a tight reach and/or you have a large group close ahead to sail over. It is essential to ensure that spinnakers are well squared around so that they are on the new leeward side on completion of the gybe.

Ideally RSA should make a high entry toward the gybe mark, gybe and pass the mark already on the new tack in order to be up high on the boat ahead's weather quarter and in a position to roll over her if possible. But she must be ready for the next manoeuvre which could well be a luff.

Round wide and gybe late to stay low. This is very effective for a second reach that is very broad, or even a run due to a backing wind, a leeward mark in the wrong place or allowing for tide/current.

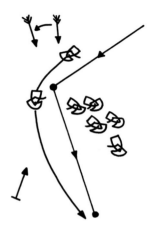

While trying to establish a late overlap, do not forget Rule 39 if the boat clear ahead tries to bear away to prevent you from doing so.

This is one of those occasions to slow down while racing and gain the advantage at both the gybe and leeward marks by cutting

across transoms for a better rounding and clearer wind.

down the fleet to gain more points. This may occur in both fleet and team racing.

Summary: Concentration during a reaching leg must be as good as at any other time during the race in order to gain a tactical advantage and maintain boat speed.

Tactics during a running leg

Race strategy: If there was a favoured side

Here is an opportunity, using Rules 37 and 39, if it is necessary to take an opponent

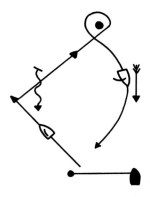

Leaving the leeward mark to port, GBR has worked out to the left nicely to protect herself for clear wind and prevented JPN from getting a late overlap. Good downwind tactics.

to go up the beat, then there will be a favoured side to go down the run due to the wind, tide/current or sea state.

In shifty conditions, ensure that you start the running leg in sequence with the wind shifts:

A If high on starboard tack when approaching the windward mark (marks to port), gybe immediately.

B If low, bear away first.

Generally speaking, the stronger the wind, the flatter you can sail down the run (straight down the rhumb line). In light winds you will have to sail slightly higher to maintain speed; this is more pronounced in catamarans and the heavier keel boats.

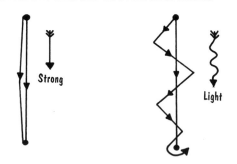

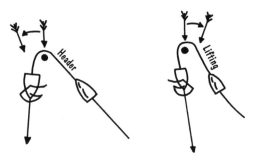

On short running legs, as a leader, stay outside the blanket wind zone to maintain speed over those trapped in the zone, then cut in on a faster point of sailing at the end of the run.

Keeping all these points in mind, the key tactical manoeuvres to look out for on a running leg are as follows:

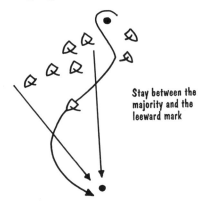

Stay between the majority and the leeward mark

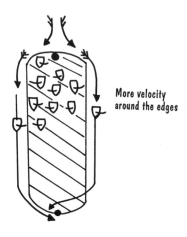

More velocity around the edges

When leading, stay between the opposition and the leeward mark whichever way they go.

Thereafter you must concentrate on:

- Clear wind
- Boat speed
- Tacking angles downwind to maintain boat speed

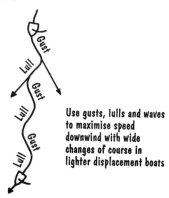

Use gusts, lulls and waves to maximise speed downwind with wide changes of course in lighter displacement boats

Use the gusts; bear away in them, and come up in the lulls. Likewise, use the waves: bear away down their faces and luff up in the troughs. Gybe with the wind shifts.

Towards the end of the leg, and if close to others, start looking for the overlap(s) and the inside berth when rounding the mark. Don't forget to allow for different angles of approach by other boats when establishing overlaps.

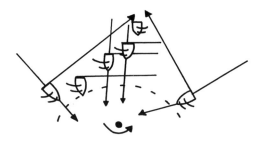

To make the best rounding at speed, the final approach to the mark should be wide and must be on the correct tack with a narrow exit from the mark.

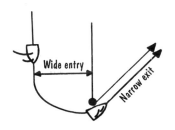

Wide entry

Narrow exit

As an attacking boat from clear astern, in order to close the gap this vessel must gybe on top of the leader all the time to take their wind and also to try to make them make a mistake. Making this leg last longer improves their chances of closing the gap and getting an overlap at the leeward mark.

Gybe inside and on top all the time to close the gap

Using Rule 37, take them out to the lay line before gybing and securing your inside berth, or be clear ahead as you round.

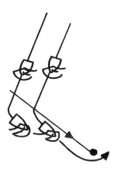

Summary: Running tactics are equally as exciting as on any other leg of the course. Think about your options and grab the chances as and when you can. These situations do tend to develop very quickly, so – like a good chess player – always be a few moves ahead in your mind to gain the advantage at the right time as the opportunities arise.

9

The Racing Rules

There are 78 Racing Rules (not forgetting Rule 79.1 – Jim needs a drink!). In many sports and games, rules can be used as weapons of attack and defence, and this is certainly the case in sailing. It is, therefore, essential that you have a thorough knowledge of these rules if you wish to be successful at all levels of competition.

In the past, the standard of knowledge of the rules has been poor. Why? Because racing at club level, and even at open meetings and national championships, has not encouraged the use of rules. The majority of incidents in these races go unchallenged, to be sorted out over a drink at the bar afterwards, with no action being taken. Therefore no one is any the wiser at the end as to who was right or wrong, and consequently the following weekend the same mistakes are made all over again. Unfortunately, this eventually filters through to international level, and then it is a case of frantically trying to learn the rules because we had not bothered at the lower levels. Many people do not realise the implications of Fundamental Rule D, and then wonder why they end up with a Rule 75 hearing against them. Fundamental Rule D must be read and fully understood as with all the Fundamental Rules.

Fundamental Rules

A Rendering Assistance
Every yacht shall render all possible assistance to any vessel or person in peril when in a position to do so.

B Competitors' Responsibilities
It shall be the sole responsibility of each yacht to decide whether or not to *start* or continue to *race*. By participating in a race conducted under these rules, each competitor and yacht owner agrees:
   (i) to be governed by the *rules*;
   (ii) to accept the penalties imposed and other action taken in accordance with the *rules*, subject to the appeal and review procedures provided in them as the final determination of any matter arising under the *rules*; and
   (iii) with respect to such a determination, not to resort to any court or tribunal not provided by the *rules*.

C Fair Sailing
A yacht, her owner and crew shall compete only by *sailing*, using their speed and skill, and, except in team racing, by individual effort, in compliance with the *rules* and in accordance with recognised principles of fair play and sportsmanship. A yacht may be penalised under this rule only in the case of a clear-cut violation of the above principles and only when no other *rule* applies, except Rule 75.

D Accepting Penalties
A yacht that realises she has infringed a *rule* while *racing* shall either retire promptly or accept an alternative penalty when so prescribed in the Sailing Instructions.

There are 66 rules, 78 by number because of spare numbers. The good news is that by 1997 there may only be approximately

This is not the time to hit the mark with the rest of the world close behind. Tough luck? Do a 360 degree penalty turn and get on with the race, trying to make up places. **Never give up!**

twelve rules, as the IYRU are under mounting pressure from the racing public around the world to greatly reduce the number of rules.

The rules are one of the eleven aspects of our sport. You can be excellent in the other ten, but lose an event because your knowledge of the rules is poor. *Not good enough*! Many an event has been won or lost in the protest room, so make sure you do your best not to be a casualty in that department. This is a very important part of your race training programme. It is also a good idea, whenever you have the opportunity, to go into a protest hearing for the experience – so that when it comes to the more important events in your racing career, you will know what to expect.

Learning the Racing Rules

There are numerous books on the Racing Rules, most of which are useful. However, one book in particular is a necessity for racing in the UK and that is RYA Publication YR/1. This is the only book that includes the RYA prescriptions for racing in the UK, and it is a must for all clubs and competitors.

The rules can be broken down into six parts, all of which require particular attention. For easier learning, it is recommended that you take them in the following order:

PART 1: The Definitions: There are 26 definitions and you must know them all; if you don't, you will not be able to understand the rules and use them.

PART 2: Race management. Knowledge of the Sailing Instructions and signals that can be used by the Chief Race Officer.

PART 3: General requirements of you as the boatowner before you can race your craft.

PART 4: Rules that always apply while racing.

PART 5: Other rules that apply to pre-race, the race and post-race.

PART 6: Protests and appeals.

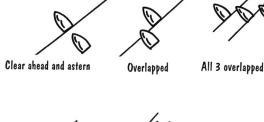

Clear ahead and astern   Overlapped   All 3 overlapped

PART 1: The Definitions
(those relevant to the race track)

1 *Abandonment*
An *abandoned* race is one that is declared void at any time and that may be resailed.

2 *Bearing Away*
Altering course away from the wind until a yacht begins to *gybe*.

Overlapped   1 & 2 overlap, 2 & 3 overlap 1 & 3 do not

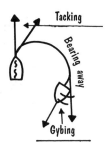

3 *Clear Astern and Clear Ahead; Overlap*
A yacht is *clear astern* of another when her hull and equipment in normal position are above an imaginary line projected abeam from the aftermost point of the other's hull and equipment in normal position. The other yacht is *clear ahead*.

The yachts *overlap* when neither is *clear astern*, or when, although one is *clear astern*, an intervening yacht *overlaps* both of them.

The terms *clear astern, clear ahead* and *overlap* apply to yachts on opposite *tacks* only when they are subject to Rule 42. For the purposes of Rules 39.1, 39.2 and 40 only: an *overlap* does not exist unless the yachts are clearly within two overall lengths of the longer yacht, and an *overlap* that exists when the *leeward yacht* starts, or when one

or both yachts completes a *tack* or a *gybe*, shall be regarded as a new overlap beginning at that time.

4 *Finishing*
A yacht *finishes* when any part of her hull, or of her crew or equipment in normal position, crosses the finishing line in the direction of the course from the last *mark*, after fulfilling any penalty obligations under Rule 52.2(b).

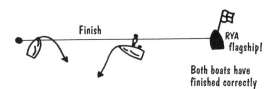

Finish   RYA flagship!

Both boats have finished correctly

5 *Gybing*
A yacht begins to *gybe* at the moment when, with the wind aft, the foot of her mainsail crosses her centreline, and completes the *gybe* when the mainsail has filled on the other *tack*.

6 *Leeward and Windward*
The *leeward* side of a yacht is that on which she is, or when head-to-wind was, carrying her mainsail. The opposite side is the *windward* side.

When neither of two yachts on the same *tack* is *clear astern*, and one on the *leeward* side of the other is the *leeward yacht*. The other is the *windward yacht*.

7 *Luffing*
Altering course towards the wind.

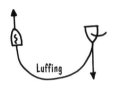

8 *Mast Abeam*
A *windward yacht sailing* no higher than a *leeward yacht* is *mast abeam* when her helmsman's line of sight abeam from his normal station is forward of the *leeward yacht's* mainmast. A *windward yacht sailing* higher than a *leeward yacht* is *mast abeam* when her helmsman's line of sight abeam from his normal station would be, if she were *sailing* no higher, forward of the *leeward yacht's* mainmast.

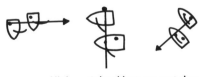

All three windward boats are mast abeam

9 *Obstruction*
An *obstruction* is any object, including a vessel under way, large enough to require a yacht, when more than one overall length away from it, to make a substantial alteration of course to pass on one side or the other, or any object that can be passed on one side only, including a buoy when the yacht in question cannot safely pass between it and the shoal or the object that it marks. The Sailing Instructions may prescribe that a specified area shall rank as an *obstruction*.

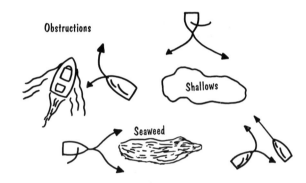

10 *Proper Course*
A *proper course* is any course that a yacht might *sail* after the starting signal, in the absence of the other yacht or yachts affected, to *finish* as quickly as possible. There is no *proper course* before the starting signal.

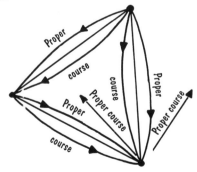

11 *Starting*

A yacht *starts* when, after fulfilling her penalty obligations, if any, under Rule 51.1(c), and after her starting signal, part of her hull, crew or equipment first crosses the starting line in the direction of the course to the first *mark*.

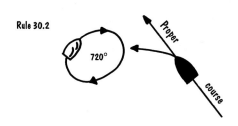

Rule 30.2

Started when after the signal you first cross the line. Both boats have started

12 *Tacking*

A yacht is *tacking* from the moment she is beyond head-to-wind until she has *borne away* to a *close-hauled* course.

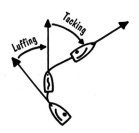

PART 4: Right-of-Way Rules

SECTION A — OBLIGATIONS AND PENALTIES

Rule 30 Hindering Another Yacht

30.1 Before or after she is *racing*, a yacht shall not seriously hinder a yacht that is *racing*.

30.2 Except when *sailing a proper course*, a

yacht shall not interfere with a yacht that is exonerating herself in accordance with Rule 52.2(a) or accepting a 720° turns penalty in accordance with Appendix B1.

Rule 31 Penalty Limitations

A yacht shall not be penalised for infringing a rule of Part 4, other than Rule 30.1, unless the infringement occurs while she is *racing*.

Rule 32 Serious Damage

When serious damage results from a collision, a yacht that had the opportunity but failed to make a reasonable attempt to avoid the collision shall be penalised.

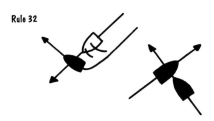

Rule 32

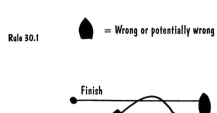

Rule 30.1 ● = Wrong or potentially wrong

Finish

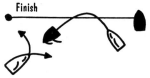

Rule 33 Contact between Yachts Racing

When there is contact between yachts *racing* that is both minor and unavoidable, the yachts shall be penalised unless:

(a) one of them lodges a valid *protest*; or

(b) one of them, or a third yacht, retires (or exonerates herself by accepting an alternative penalty when so prescribed in the Sailing Instructions) in acknowledgement of an infringement in that incident.

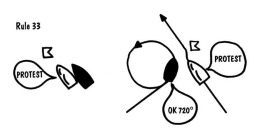

Rule 33

PROTEST

PROTEST

OK 720°

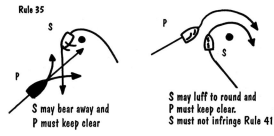

Rule 35

S may bear away and
P must keep clear

S may luff to round and
P must keep clear.
S must not infringe Rule 41

Rule 34 Retention of Rights

A yacht that may have infringed a *rule* but that is not obviously retiring or exonerating herself retains her rights under the rules of Part 4, and other yachts shall treat her accordingly.

Rule 34

W must keep clear of L until L starts to get clear to take her 360° turn

SECTION B – BASIC RIGHT-OF-WAY RULES AND THEIR LIMITATIONS

Rule 35 Limitations on Altering Course

When one yacht is required to keep clear

of another, the right-of-way yacht shall not alter course so as to prevent the other yacht from keeping clear, or so as to obstruct her while she is keeping clear, except:

(a) When *luffing* as permitted by Rule 39.2; or

(b) When assuming a *proper course either*:

(i) *to start*, when she is on the *starboard tack* and the other yacht is on the *port tack*; or

(ii) when rounding a *mark*.

Rule 36 Opposite Tacks – Basic Rules

A *port-tack* yacht shall keep clear of a starboard-tack yacht.

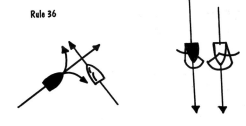

Rule 36

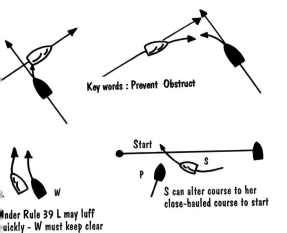

Key words : Prevent Obstruct

Start

S

P

S can alter course to her close-hauled course to start

W

Under Rule 39 L may luff quickly - W must keep clear

Rule 37 Same Tack – Basic Rules

37.1 Overlapped

A *windward yacht* shall keep clear of a *leeward* yacht.

37.2 Not Overlapped

A yacht *clear astern* shall keep clear of a yacht *clear ahead*.

37.3 Establishing an Overlap

A yacht that establishes an *overlap* to

Rule 37

leeward from *clear astern* shall initially allow the *windward yacht* ample *room* and opportunity to keep clear.

Rule 38 Same Tack – Before Clearing the Starting Line

38.1 Sailing Above a Close-Hauled Course
Before she starts and clears the starting

Pre-start Timberland has the right to luff slowly up to a close hauled course and head to wind and the boat to windward has to keep clear hoping to force her over the line at the start.

line, a *leeward yacht* shall not *sail* above her *close-hauled course when the windward yacht* is *mast abeam* and would have to alter course to keep clear.

38.2 Luffing
Before she starts and clears the starting

Rule 38.1

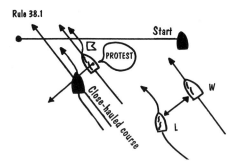

L may luff above close-hauled
as it does not affect W

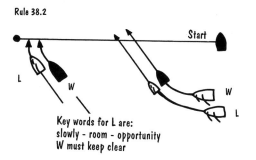

Rule 38.2

Start

L

W

W

L

Key words for L are:
slowly - room - opportunity
W must keep clear

line, when a *leeward yacht* or a yacht *clear ahead luffs* so that another yacht will have to alter course to keep clear, she shall *luff* only slowly, and initially in such a way as to give the *windward yacht room* and opportunity to keep clear.

Rule 39 Same Tack – After Clearing the Starting Line

39.1 Sailing Above a Proper Course

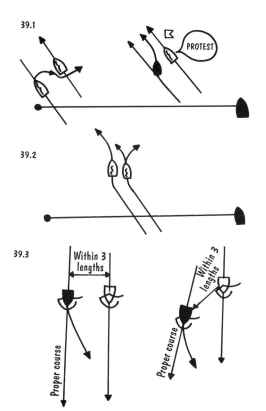

39.1

PROTEST

39.2

39.3

Within 3 lengths

Within 3 lengths

Proper course

Proper course

After *starting* and clearing the starting line, when a *windward yacht* has been *mast abeam* at any time during the *overlap*, the *leeward yacht* shall not *sail* above her *proper course* unless she *luffs* and *tacks* without interfering with the *windward yacht*.

39.2 Luffing

After *starting* and clearing the starting line, subject to Rule 32, a yacht *clear ahead* or a *leeward yacht* may *luff* as she pleases unless the *windward yacht* has been *mast abeam* at any time during the *overlap*.

39.3 Sailing Below a Proper Course

A yacht on a free leg of the course shall not *sail* below her *proper course* when she is within three of her overall lengths of a *leeward yacht* or of a yacht *clear astern* that is steering a course to *leeward* of her, unless she *bears away* and *gybes* on to another *proper course* without interfering with the other yacht.

Rule 40 Other Limitations on a Leeward Yacht

40.1 Doubt About Mast Abeam

When there is doubt that a *windward yacht* is *mast abeam* and her helmsman hails 'Mast abeam' or words to that effect, the *leeward yacht* shall promptly comply with Rule 38.1 or Rule 39.1. When she believes the hail is improper, her only remedy is to protest.

40.2 Safety Limitation

When a *windward yacht* hails that an *obstruction*, a third yacht or other object limits her ability to keep clear when a

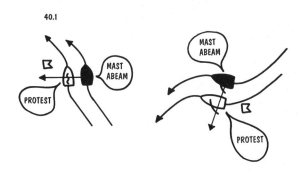

40.1

MAST ABEAM

MAST ABEAM

PROTEST

PROTEST

40.2

40.3

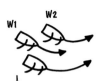

W1 W2

W2 must respond to
W1's luff even though
she does not have
luffing rights

L

leeward yacht luffs, the *leeward yacht* shall give the *windward yacht room* to pass the object.

40.3 Luffing Two or More Yachts

A *leeward yacht* shall not *luff* unless she has the right to luff all yachts that would be affected, in which case they all shall respond, including any intervening yacht that does not otherwise have the right to *luff*.

Rule 41 Changing Tacks – Tacking and Gybing

41.1 Basic Rule

A yacht that is either *tacking* or *gybing* shall keep clear of a yacht on a *tack*.

41.2 Transitional

A yacht shall neither *tack* nor *gybe* into a position that will give her right-of-way unless she does so far enough from a yacht on a *tack* to enable that yacht to keep clear without having to begin to alter her course until after the *tack* or *gybe* has been completed.

The windward boat must keep clear here until the mast abeam position has been reached when the leeward boat is obliged to bear away on to her proper course for the next mark.

Rule 41

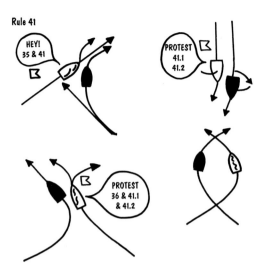

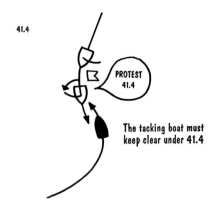

The tacking boat must keep clear under 41.4

41.3 Onus
A yacht that *tacks* or *gybes* has the onus of satisfying the *protest committee* that she completed her *tack* or *gybe* in accordance with Rule 41.2.

41.4 Tacking or Gybing at the Same Time
When two yachts are both *tacking* or both

Having arrived at the mark within two boat lengths EUN, with the inside overlap, has the right to make a good rounding in a seamanlike manner for the conditions at the time, and if she wants to edge out a bit to make a good mark rounding the outside boat must give her the room required. If there is contact between them the outside boat should be gyrating shortly afterwards or else end up in front of the protest committee – DSQ!

gybing at the same time, the one on the other's port side shall keep clear. When one yacht is *tacking* and another is *gybing* at the same time, the one that is *tacking* shall keep clear.

SECTION C – RULES THAT APPLY AT MARKS AND OBSTRUCTIONS AND OTHER EXCEPTIONS TO THE RULES OF SECTION B
When a rule of this section conflicts with a rule of Section B, it overrides the conflicting part of that rule, except that Rule 35 always applies.

Rule 42 Rounding or Passing Marks and Obstructions

Rule 42 applies when yachts are about to round or pass a *mark* on the same required side or an *obstruction* on the same side, except that it shall not apply:
(a) at a starting *mark* surrounded by navigable water (including such a *mark* that is also an *obstruction*) when approaching the starting line to *start* until clearing the starting *marks*. However, after her starting signal, a *leeward yacht* shall

42(b)

Rules 36 & 41 apply not 42

not deprive a *windward yacht* of *room* at such a *mark* by sailing either:
  (i) to windward of the compass bearing of the course to the next *mark*; or
  (ii) above *close-hauled*
(b) between two yachts on opposite tacks:
  (i) when they are on a beat; or
  (ii) when one, but not both, of them will have to tack either to round or pass the *mark* or to avoid the *obstruction*.
42.1 When Overlapped
An Outside Yacht
(a) Except as provided in Rule 42.3, an outside yacht shall give each inside *overlapping* yacht *room* to round or pass the *mark* or *obstruction*, including *room* to *tack* or *gybe* when either is an integral part of the rounding or passing manoeuvre.
(b) An outside yacht *overlapped* when she comes within two of her overall lengths of a *mark* or *obstruction* shall give *room* as required, even though the *overlap* may thereafter be broken.
(c) An outside *yacht* that claims to have broken an *overlap* has the onus of

42(a)

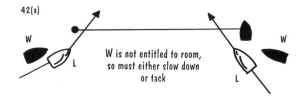

W is not entitled to room, so must either slow down or tack

42.1(a)

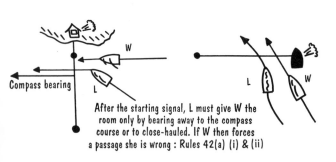

After the starting signal, L must give W the room only by bearing away to the compass course or to close-hauled. If W then forces a passage she is wrong : Rules 42(a) (i) & (ii)

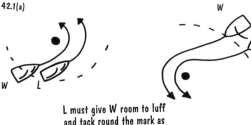

L must give W room to luff and tack round the mark as W must give L room to gybe round. 42.1(a) overrides Rule 41, as it is in Section C of Part 4. Room means enough to make a seamanlike tactical rounding for the conditions

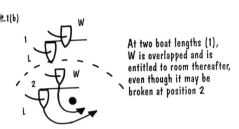

2.1(b)

At two boat lengths (1),
W is overlapped and is
entitled to room thereafter,
even though it may be
broken at position 2

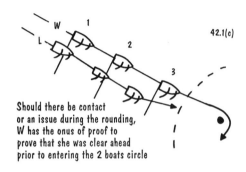

42.1(c)

Should there be contact
or an issue during the rounding,
W has the onus of proof to
prove that she was clear ahead
prior to entering the 2 boats circle

satisfying the *protest committee* that she
became *clear ahead* when she was more
than two of her overall lengths from the
mark or *obstruction*.

An Inside Yacht

(d) A yacht that claims an inside *overlap*
has the onus of satisfying the *protest*

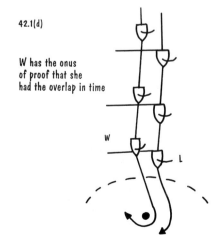

42.1(d)

W has the onus
of proof that she
had the overlap in time

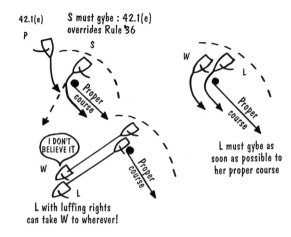

42.1(e)   S must gybe : 42.1(e)
overrides Rule 36

I DON'T
BELIEVE IT

L with luffing rights
can take W to wherever!

L must gybe as
soon as possible to
her proper course

committee that she established the *overlap*
in accordance with Rule 42.3.

(e) When an inside yacht of two or more
overlapped yachts, either on opposite
tacks or on the same *tack* without luffing
rights, will have to *gybe* in order most
directly to assume a *proper course* to the
next *mark*, she shall *gybe* at the first
reasonable opportunity.

42.2 When Not Overlapped

(a) When a yacht *clear ahead* comes
within two of her overall lengths of a *mark*
or *obstruction*, a yacht *clear astern* shall
keep clear until the yachts complete the
rounding or passing manoeuvre, provided
the yacht *clear ahead* remains on the same
tack or *gybes*. A yacht *clear ahead* is not
required to give *room* to a yacht *clear
astern* before an *overlap* is established.

(b) A yacht *clear ahead* that *tacks* to

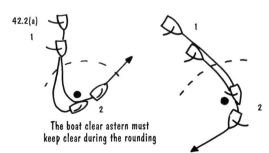

42.2(a)

The boat clear astern must
keep clear during the rounding

115

It appears that 886 has wrongly been compelled to hit the mark by boats to leeward not giving her the room to round in a seamanlike manner. If this is the case she need not do a 360 degree turn but must lodge a protest against the leeward boat, making sure that she gets the correct number. If in doubt she should do her 360 penalty and lodge a protest. At least in that way 886 could not be disqualified.

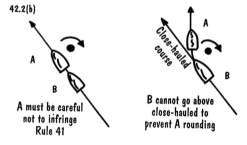

42.2(b)

A

B

A must be careful
not to infringe
Rule 41

Close-hauled course

A

B

B cannot go above
close-hauled to
prevent A rounding

round a *mark* is subject to Rule 41, but a yacht *clear astern* shall not *luff* above *close-hauled* so as to prevent her from *tacking*.

42.3 Limitations

(a) Limitation on Establishing an Overlap

A yacht that established an inside *overlap* is entitled to *room* under Rule 42.1(a) only when, at that time, the outside yacht:

(i) is able to give *room*; and

(ii) when the *overlap* is established from *clear astern*, is more than two of her overall lengths from the *mark* or *obstruction*.

However, when a yacht completes a *tack* within two of her overall lengths of a *mark* or *obstruction*, she shall give *room* as required by Rule 42.1(a) to a yacht that, by *luffing*, cannot thereafter avoid establishing a late inside *overlap*.

(b) Limitation When an Obstruction is a Continuing One

When yachts are passing a continuing *obstruction*, such as a shoal or the shore or another vessel, Rule 42.3(a)(ii) does not apply, and a yacht *clear astern* may establish an *overlap* between a yacht *clear ahead* and the *obstruction*, provided, at that time, there is *room* for her to pass between them in safety.

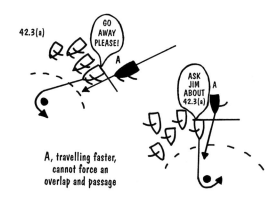

42.3(a)

GO AWAY PLEASE!

A

ASK JIM ABOUT 42.3(a) A

A, travelling faster, cannot force an overlap and passage

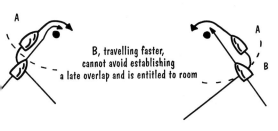

A

B, travelling faster, cannot avoid establishing a late overlap and is entitled to room

A

B

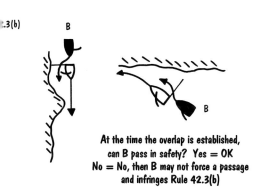

.3(b)

B

B

At the time the overlap is established, can B pass in safety? Yes = OK
No = No, then B may not force a passage and infringes Rule 42.3(b)

Rule 43 Close-hauled, Hailing for Room to Tack at Obstructions

43.1 Hailing

When two yachts are on the same *tack* and the yacht *clear ahead* or the *leeward yacht* is *close-hauled*, and safe pilotage requires her to make a substantial alteration of course to clear an *obstruction*, and when she intends to *tack*, but cannot *tack* without colliding with the other yacht, she shall hail the other yacht for *room* to *tack* and clear the other yacht, but she shall not hail and *tack* simultaneously.

43.2 Responding

The hailed yacht at the earliest possible moment after the hail shall either:

(a) *tack*, in which case the hailing yacht shall begin to *tack* as soon as she is able to *tack* and clear the other yacht; or

(b) reply 'You *tack*' or words to that effect, in which case:

(i) the hailing yacht shall immediately *tack* and

(ii) the hailed yacht shall give the hailing yacht *room* to *tack* and clear her;

(iii) the onus of satisfying the *protest committee* that she gave sufficient *room* shall lie on the hailed yacht that replied 'You *tack*'.

43.3 When an Obstruction Is Also a Mark

(a) When an *obstruction* is a starting *mark* surrounded by navigable water, or the ground tackle of such a *mark*, and when approaching the starting line to *start* and after *starting*, the yacht *clear ahead* or the *leeward yacht* shall not be entitled to *room* to tack.

(b) At other *obstructions* that are *marks*, when the hailed yacht can fetch the

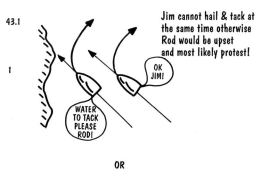

43.1

1

WATER TO TACK PLEASE ROD!

OK JIM!

Jim cannot hail & tack at the same time otherwise Rod would be upset and most likely protest!

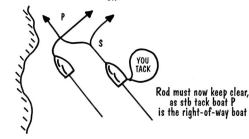

OR

2

P

S

YOU TACK

Rod must now keep clear, as stb tack boat P is the right-of-way boat

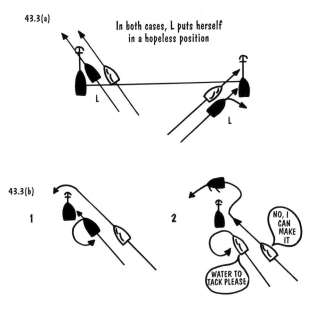

43.3(a)

In both cases, L puts herself in a hopeless position

43.3(b)

1

2

NO, I CAN MAKE IT

WATER TO TACK PLEASE

Rule 45 Keeping Clear after Touching a Mark

A yacht that has touched a *mark* and is exonerating herself shall keep clear of all other yachts until she has completed her exoneration and, when she has *started*, is on a *proper course* to the next *mark*.

45

360°

360°

You must keep clear while exonerating until on your proper course

obstruction, the hailing yacht shall not be entitled to *room* to *tack* and clear the hailed yacht, and the hailed yacht shall immediately so inform the hailing yacht. When the hailed yacht then fails to fetch, she shall retire or accept an alternative penalty when so prescribed in the Sailing Instructions.

Rule 44 On the Course Side of the Starting Line

After her starting signal, a yacht that has not *started* and is sailing toward the pre-start side of the starting line or its extensions shall, until wholly on its pre-start side, keep clear of yachts that have *started* or are on the pre-start side. She shall then give any newly obligated yacht ample *room* and opportunity to keep clear.

Rule 46 Person Overboard: Yacht Anchored, Aground or Capsized

46.1 A yacht under way shall keep clear of another yacht *racing* that:
(a) is manoeuvring or hailing for the purpose of rescuing a person overboard; or
(b) is anchored, aground or capsized.
46.2 A yacht shall not be penalised when she is unable to avoid fouling a yacht that she is attempting to assist or that goes aground or is capsized.
46.3 A yacht is capsized from the time her masthead is in the water until her masthead is clear of the water and she has steerage way.

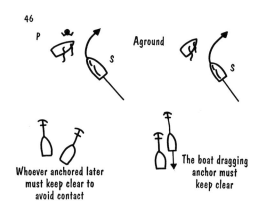

46

P

Aground

S

S

Whoever anchored later must keep clear to avoid contact

The boat dragging anchor must keep clear

44

Start

S

S

P

S must keep clear and give P room and opportunity to keep clear

46.4 A yacht anchored or aground shall indicate the fact to any yacht that may be in danger of fouling her. Under normal conditions, a hail is sufficient indication. Of two yachts anchored, the one that anchored later shall keep clear, except that a yacht dragging shall keep clear of one that is not.

The following are some examples of when a starboard-tack boat does not have right of way over a port-tack boat while racing:

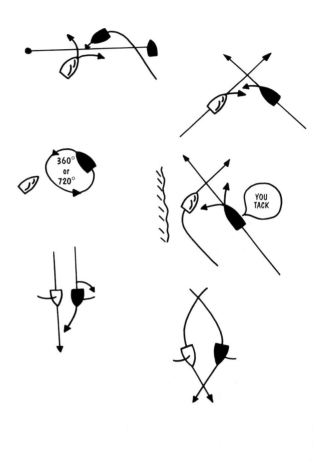

Occasions when stb tack
does not have right of way over port

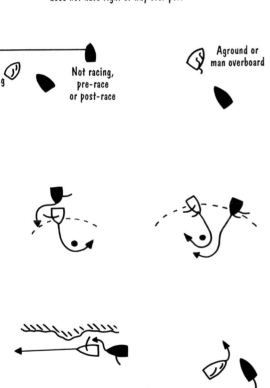

Not racing,
pre-race
or post-race

Aground or
man overboard

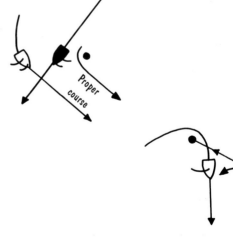

Proper course

PART 5: Other Sailing Rules

There are some interesting situations in Part V of the rules which are worth looking at as these are very often forgotten by competitors at hectic moments in a race.

Rule 51.1 (c)

This rule addresses Flag I - the one minute round-the-ends rule. If Flag I is not flown and there is an individual recall, which you believe refers to you, then you do not need to go round either end; just stop your boat, let those either side of you pass, return to the line, dip it, look for Flag X to be lowered and start correctly. This is the quickest way of getting back into the race if you have not started near either end of the line. However, if you are near an end it may well be as quick to either bear away and gybe round the port end or tack and go round the starboard end. The only problem you may have by dipping the line in the middle, as suggested, is if there is more than one boat over the line. In this event you may return, think that you have crossed and cleared the line but that Flag X is still raised because others have not yet returned and cleared. You must therefore make absolutely certain that you have cleared the line before turning back or you may find yourself with a PMS in the results. It extraordinary how many boats when recalled go round the ends from an area in the middle of the line when the one minute rule is not in force, so please do not forget it.

Another situation worth looking at under Rule 51 is 51.1 (D) which refers to individual recalls, Flag X and no sound signal. It is mandatory that Flag X be accompanied by a sound signal to draw competitors' attention to the fact that there is an individual recall and that one or more boats are over the line at start time. If there is no sound signal there is no onus on a yacht to return and start correctly unless it is obvious to an individual that he is over. In this event he is subject to Fundamental Rule 'D' and must return to start correctly.

Rule 52.1 (A111)

This rule is one that is very often forgotten or not even known by many competitors and refers to finishing and in particular contact with the finishing mark. Do not forget that if you finish close to a finishing mark and hit it as you are clearing the finishing line, you have in fact unfinished yourself. You must do your 360° penalty turn and return to the course side of the finishing line in order to finish the race correctly. Many times I have seen a competitor hit the finishing mark as he crosses the finishing line and think that it is of no consequence as he has already finished the race, only to discover later a DNF on the results sheet.

Rule 54

Generally speaking I think that most competitors have come to terms with Rule 54 and understand its meanings. However, one part worth mentioning is sculling. If, in very light winds with no steerageway on the boat, you wish to either luff or bear away, a helm hard over being sculled in a corner to turn the bast is permissable as this is being done to steer the boat and not to propel it forward.

Appendix B1.
Alternative Penalties: 720 degree turn.

The 720° turn is commonly used in small boat racing at all levels of competition and competitors are fully aware of this procedure. However, unfortunately some competitors collect another penalty for not doing to correctly.

Here are some guide lines to follow:

- Firstly, you can only exonerate yourself with a 720° turn if you have infringed a Rule in Part IV of the Rule Book

- Secondly, if you think you have or have definitely infringed a Rule of Part IV you must complete your turns as soon as possible after the incident, keeping well clear of those racing. Do your two full turns, both in the same direction remembering that whichever tack you started on you must finish on. Do not make the mistake of only doing a 630° turn and being protested against again!! It is also worth remembering that if your incident involves hitting a mark, it is not necessary to do another 360° turn as your 720° turn is sufficient. ·

- As the protestor, it is worth remembering that although you are obliged to see the protestee start to take the penalty, it is not necessary for you to see him complete it. However, if you do not see the penalty completed you must lodge your protest at the finish vessel, if required by the sailing instructions, until it has been established as a fact that the 720° turn was done and the 720° form signed accordingly if applicable (SI's). It has been known for a protestee to have only done 360° turn but then signed the 720° form. This has resulted in him being protested against and then hit with a Rule 75 hearing. So be very careful about what you see and do.

- Two further points to remember about 720° turns: If you infringe a rule during the pre-start period you can do your turn immediately and do not have to wait until after the starting signal. If an incident occurs at the finish you may carry out your penalty turn on either side of the finishing line but you must return to the course side of this line to then finish the race.

So, plenty to be constantly thinking about with regard to the rules. Focus on them and concentrate fully especially in the starting area, during mark roundings and passing situations as there is much to be gained and lost in this department. This is why it is a very important part of your training programme in preparation for your events.

Protests and hearings

Mention the word 'protest' and most people immediately react with 'You 'orrible person' or similar inner thoughts! However, this is the wrong attitude to adopt towards 'protests'. There is nothing nasty about lodging a protest when you firmly believe that another boat (or boats) has infringed a rule or a Sailing Instruction. After all, in normal club and fleet racing there is no 'on the water' referee to blow a whistle and show a yellow or red card, as there is in match racing and some team racing events. Our sport is very much a self-policing one, and it has to be conducted in that manner by all competitors for otherwise it would degenerate into a waste of time, money and effort.

So *who* can protest? The answer is that any yacht can protest any other yacht. For a protest under a rule of Part 4 of the Racing Rules, a yacht can only protest another yacht if she is directly involved in, or is witness to, the incident.

Under Rule 68.2, if during a race you are directly involved in an incident you must immediately inform the other yacht by clearly displaying your protest flag and hailing 'Protest'. In all other cases, if you intend to protest you must inform the protested yacht at the first reasonable opportunity.

It is important to remember that if you are directly involved you must inform immediately in order to give the protested yacht the opportunity to carry out her 720° turn – if applicable. It is also worth remembering that, if you protest but are not absolutely sure that you are within your rights to do so, you as the protestor can also do a 720° turn as well as lodge a protest, which will protect you against being disqualified if the other boat does a 720° turn but protests you. (This applies unless there are other complications, ie Rule 32.)

Please don't forget the requirement of flying your protest flag immediately after the incident and to keep it flying under Rule 68.3. In the case of singlehanders, you still have the right under the new rules to display it, put it away, and display it again to the race committee at the finishing line. On trapezing boats I would recommend a flag on each trapeze wire for the crew to display as soon as possible, as you cannot come in off the wire to find the flag!

Rule 69 Requests for redress

An important fact to note is that you do not need to fly a protest flag to seek redress, under this rule. You may only seek redress under the following headings:

A an improper action or omission of either the race or protest committee.

B when you have assisted someone under Fundamental Rule 'A'.

C when you have been damaged by another vessel that was required to keep clear of you.

D infringing Fundamental Rule 'C'.

Action by the race or protest committee under Rule 70.2.

This is an interesting rule to remember. It adds to Rule 68.1 as both the race and protest committee may call a hearing when:

1 they see an infringement of the Racing Rules or Sailing Instructions:

2 they learn directly by either a written or verbal statement from a yacht that she may either have infringed a rule or Sailing Instruction;

3 they learn directly from a yacht's invalid protest that she herself has infringed Rules 33 or 52.1, and did not exonerate herself;

4 either the race or the protest committee has reasonable grounds for believing that an

infringement resulted in serious damage; or receives a report, not later than on the same day of the race, from a witness, who was neither competing or is an interested party, alleging an infringement of a rule or Sailing Instruction; or has reasonable grounds for supposing from the evidence of a valid protest that any yacht involved in an incident may have infringed a rule or Sailing Instruction.

Key points to remember about protests:

- Immediately hail 'Protest' (not 720 or anything else!).
- Immediately fly your protest flag (unless it is impossible to do so, when you will be invited to say why you did not do so). But make sure that you have an excellent reason, otherwise you will have an invalid protest on your hands.
- Remember the sail number of the boat you are protesting against. If you bring the wrong boat into a hearing you will again have an invalid protest.
- Initially observe whether or not the protestee begins to do a 720° turn (if applicable). If not, go ahead with your protest. (You do not have to witness the conclusion of the 720°).
- Notify the committee boat at the finish of the race that you intend to protest, and against which boat. This is usually a requirement of the Sailing Instructions.
- Fill out your protest form neatly that the committee can clearly understand it and hand it in within the allotted time for protests to be lodged (check noticeboard); if you don't do this, you may be subject to a third party protest who witnessed the incident.
- Meet with any witnesses, go through their evidence, make sure that they appear in the right place at the right time.
- Before going into the hearing, be sure that you are looking presentable. It is

surprising how first impressions can count with a Jury or Protest Committee. Take in with you a pen, paper, Rule Book and Interpretations.

- State your case only when invited to do so by the chairman. Make it short, and to the point: no 'ifs', 'maybes', 'I think so', or 'I'm not sure'. Use models accurately, and when they are in position move your hands out of the way to enable the Protest Committee and the protestee to see them clearly.
- Make notes while you are listening to the protestee's case, and if there are any discrepancies in this presentation you will be able to identify them and use them when cross-examining in order to place an element of doubt in the committee's mind.
- After the main part of the hearing you will be asked to sum up your case. Reinforce your opening statement from the information gained during the hearing. Once again, keep it short, sweet and to the point, referring to the rule numbers that you consider have been infringed. The less you need to say in presenting your case, the better.
  Never interrupt either the jury or the protestor/ee. And never lie – always remember that Rule 75 is lurking around the corner.
- After the decision – win or lose – always shake hands with your opponent and the protest committee, and be polite at all times. This will go in your favour if and when you meet the same committee/jury members at future events.

Remember, even if you are certain and confident that you were in the right on the water at the time of the incident, when you actually go into the protest room it is a 50/50 scenario, and you could come out having lost if you do not present your case well. Protest hearings can be won or lost on their presentation and by the way you conduct yourself at the hearing, and it is very worthwhile getting together with a crew

or friend and practising the procedures, especially before attending international events with international juries. Appearing for the first time before an international jury can be very daunting, so if you get the opportunity to do so – perhaps as a witness if not an actual protestor – make the most of it; it is all good experience.

Rules 71–74 – Protest procedure

As a competitor, the key points for you to remember under the protest rules are as follows:

- You cannot be penalised without a hearing unless you are subject to Rule 70.1
- No member of a protest committee shall take part in discussions or decisions in which they are an interested party. They can, however, give evidence.
- If a protestor or protestee believes that a member of the protest committee is an interested party, then they must say so to the chairman before evidence commences or as soon as possible when you believe there is a conflict of interest.
- If you are involved in an incident with a boat from another race, your hearing will be conducted by a combined protest committee from two organising clubs.
- Once notified of a protest, the protestee must receive a copy of the protest and be allowed the time to prepare a defence; if this does not happen, you as the protestee may request that the hearing be postponed until you have had this opportunity.
- Should you fail to attend the hearing, a protest committee has the right to proceed without you and make a decision, so make sure that you do attend the hearing.
- *Reopening a hearing*: a hearing can only be reopened for the following reasons:
  (a) If the protest committee believes that they have made an error of judgement.
  (b) When new evidence becomes

available within reasonable time.
(c) When directed to do so by the National Authority under Rule 77.4 (Appeals).

A protestor or protestee may request a hearing to be reopened for reasons (a) or (b) above before 1800 hours the day after the original decision, unless the protest committee has good reason to extend this time limit. Should a protest committee wish to reopen a hearing after 1800 hours the following day because *they* believe that *they* made an error of judgement, they may do so within reasonable time. Please remember that a request to reopen a hearing is not automatically granted. A protest committee shall reach a decision based on the *facts found* – There can be no appeal against the *facts found*, only on an interpretation of the rules, the procedures for which are found under Rules 77–78. (Interesting reading is Appendix C1, Protest Committee Procedure, in the Rule Book.)

Many mistakes are made over the subject of protests, primarily because of competitors' lack of knowledge of Rules 68–78 and/or Appendix C1. Therefore I would thoroughly recommend some careful homework in this area before taking part in any important events.

It amazes me just how many competitors are caught out by a third party protest. If you are a third party yacht witnessing an incident, you must remember that in order to have a valid protest, you, as the third party, *must* fly a protest flag if neither of the other yachts fly one. Also, do not forget time limits for protests, because if you are late in lodging your protest you could be subject to a third party protest either from the jury/protest committee or another competitor. Protests and procedures are equally as important in your race preparation as all the other aspects of the sport, so you should therefore take time to study them.

Protest committee procedure

It is important for you, as a competitor, to know what to expect when you go into a protest hearing. The format and procedure is as follows:

1 Preliminaries
1.1 Preliminaries are completed by the jury secretary, race committee or *protest committee* as circumstances dictate.
1.2 Note on the protest form the time it is received.
1.3 Notify the representative of each yacht involved, and the race committee when appropriate, of the time and place of the hearing (Rule 72).
1.4 Make available the protest form and any written statement regarding the incident (preferably photocopies) to all *parties to the protest* and each member of the *protest committee* for study before the hearing begins. Allow a reasonable time for the preparation of a defence (Rule 72).

2 The Protest Committee
2.1 Make sure that a quorum is present when required by the organising authority. The quorum is not affected when some members of the committee leave the hearing during the discussion and decision at the request of the committee.
2.2 Make sure that no *interested party* is a member of the *protest committee*. When the hearing starts, ask the *parties to the protest* whether they object to any member on the grounds of 'interest' (Rule 71.2).
2.3 When the *protest* involves a question of redress under Rule 69(a) and involves a member of the race committee, that person does not serve as a member of the *protest committee*, but may appear as a witness.

3 The Validity of the Protest
3.1 At the beginning of the hearing, determine whether the *protest* contains the information called for by Rule 68.5, provided it already identifies the incident (Rule 68.7). If not, ask the protestor to

supply the information (Rule 68.7). When the *protest* does not identify the nature of the incident, it is refused (Rule 73.2).

3.2 Unless the *protest* already provides the information:

(a) when the protestor was involved in the incident, ask whether the protestor hailed the protested yacht immediately in accordance with Rule 68.2; when no hail was required, ask whether the protestor tried to inform the protestee that a protest would be lodged (Rule 68.2);

(b) ask whether the protestor displayed a protest flag in accordance with Rule 68.3, unless Rule 68.4 applies or the protestor is seeking redress under Rule 69, and note his answer on the protest form.

3.3 When a protest flag has not been properly displayed or a hail not made, or an attempt not made to inform the protestee when required, the protest is refused (Rule 73.2), except when the *protest committee* decides either that:

(a) Rule 68.4 applies, or

(b) it was impossible for the yacht to have displayed a protest flag because she was, for example, dismasted, capsized or sunk.

4 Evidence and Statements

4.1 One representative of each *party to the protest* (with a language interpreter when needed) has the right to be present throughout the hearing. When appropriate, make sure that the representative has been on board. Witnesses are excluded except when giving their evidence. Observers may be admitted at the discretion of the *protest committee* (Rule 73.1).

4.2 Invite the protestor and then the protestee(s) to give their accounts of the incident. Each may question the other(s). Questions by the *protest committee*, except for clarifying details, are preferably deferred until all accounts have been presented. Models are useful; the positions of the yachts before and after the incident are often helpful.

4.3 Invite the protestor and then the protestee(s) to call witnesses (Rule 73). They may be questioned by the parties as well as by the *protest committee*. The *protest committee* may also call witnesses. An *interested party* may give evidence (Rule 71.2(a)), but it may be appropriate and prudent to ask a witness to disclose any business or other relationship through which he might have an interest, or might stand to benefit from the outcome of the *protest*.

4.4 When any member of the *protest committee* saw the incident, his evidence is given as a witness only in the presence of the *parties to the protest*, and he may be questioned (Rule 73.4).

4.5 Invite first the protestor and then the protestee to make a final statement of his case, including any application or interpretation of the *rules* he thinks useful.

4.6 A hearing may be adjourned in order to obtain additional evidence.

4.7 When one of the parties has been notified (Rule 72), but made no effort to attend the hearing (Rule 73.5), the *protest* may be heard without that person. Make careful notes on any steps taken to try to find the person concerned. When the protestee is absent, hear the evidence of the protestor and question him or her before imposing a penalty.

5 Decision

5.1 After dismissing the *parties to the protest*, decide what the relevant facts are (Rule 74.1).

5.2 Apply the *rules* and reach a decision as to which yacht, if any, infringed a *rule*, and which *rule* was infringed (Rule 74).

5.3 Having reached a decision and recorded it, recall the *parties to the protest* and read them the facts found, the decision, and the grounds for it (Rule 74.6).

5.4 Any *party to the protest* is entitled to a copy of the decision (Rule 74.6). A copy is also filed with the committee records.

6 Reopening a hearing

When a timely request is made for a hearing to be reopened (Rule 73.6), hear how the committee may have made a significant error and investigate the evidence (eg see the video tape or question the witness) and decide whether it is material that could change the decision. If none of these apply, refuse to reopen; otherwise, call the hearing.

Rule 69 Requests for redress

Where the RYA has jurisdiction over events, (ie those held within the United Kingdom) appeals can be made for a hearing by the Racing Rules Committee by initially contacting the RYA Racing Manager. Elsewhere in the world they would be submitted to the host country's governing body of the sport.

An appeal against the decision of a Protest Committee is usually made because either the Protestor or Protestee believe that the Protest Committee have made an error in their judgement. On receiving such an appeal, the Racing Rules Committee will study the evidence provided and may alter the Protest Committee's decision. You may also appeal to a National Authority when you believe that a protest hearing should have been opened for all the valid reasons but was not.

Finally, you can also appeal if you believe that, after seeking redress under Rule 69, none was received when you felt that you were entitled to it.

Who Can Appeal:
1 Protestor
2 Protestee
3 Any penalised yacht
4 Protest refused
5 Re-hearing refused
6 Request for redress refused
7 Penalised under Rule 75
8 Protest Committee – when not sure of its own decision

9 Race Committee – against the decision of its own Protest Committee

Appeal Procedure – Rule 78

Once you have been given the Protest Committee's decision in writing you have 15 days in which you can lodge your appeal to the appropriate National Authority. Your appeal must include the following:

- Your reasons for making the appeal
- A copy of the Protest Committee's decision
- Any fee required by the National Authority (£35 in the case of the RYA).
- Protest form(s)
- A diagram of the incident
- Any written statements submitted by Protestor or Protestee
- Any additional relevant documents
- Names and addresses of the chairman of the Protest Committee and parties to the protest

The National Authority will inform the Protest Committee, Protestor and Protestee that a valid appeal has been received and collect/despatch any relevant documentation not received by any of the parties concerned. An appeal can be withdrawn if after further consideration the appellant accepts the original decision of the Protest Committee.

Reasons for an appeal

- Incorrect decisions
- Procedural errors
- You can appeal against the interpretation of a rule(s) but you cannot appeal against the facts found by a Protest Committee.
- The hearing of an invalid protest may be appealed against
- You may appeal against the Protest Committee's decision for finding your protest to be invalid when you believe that it is valid and they have not heard your reasons for this.

- When your request for redress is denied and/or you believe that the request granted was not equitable either to yourself or others involved.

Right of appeal

You have no right of appeal (Rules 1.5 A & B) against a decision when it has been made by an International Jury constituted in accordance with Appendix A5 of the International Yacht Racing Rules. In addition you cannot appeal when, in the notice of race for an event and the sailing instructions, it is stated that the 'Right to appeal is denied'. This would usually occur when it is essential that the result of a particular event is known immediately because such a result may qualify a yacht to compete in a future event. Also a National Authority can so prescribe for a particular event open to entrants under its own jurisdiction: eg National Championships being used for selection trials.

An appeal authority may or may not uphold your appeal, it can also direct a Protest Committee to re-open your hearing or reinstate you or give redress. It can also penalise another yacht involved in the case and it can direct the Protest Committee to hear a case when it had decided not to.

It is also worth mentioning at this stage that an appeal can take some time to be heard, perhaps weeks or months depending on the amount of time it takes to collate the necessary information and how soon the Racing Rules Committee is due to meet. So be patient, or better still, hope that your case never needs to go to appeal and can be resolved by the Protest Committee.

10

Compass Work

As the kicking strap is probably the most important boat tuning control in the vessel, so the compass is probably the most important tactical piece of equipment in the boat.

Over the years, I have been amazed at the number of sailors who either did not know how to use a compass when racing, or have felt that they did not need to know how to use one. This has usually been the case with sailors who have mainly raced in landlocked areas. Unfortunately, when these people then have to race on open sea venues for their National, European or World Championships, they cannot understand why they sometimes don't have very good results. Often the reason for this is because they lack the knowledge of how to use a compass to establish the following key points in the race area:

- Race area orientation
- Tacking angle for the conditions
- Wind shift tracking
- Transits
- Wind shifts to windward and running
- Wind bends
- Course leg bearings

Race area orientation

When you are racing on an open sea venue anywhere in the world you will find it very useful to take to sea with you a scaled-down chart of the race area in a waterproof laminated sheet. Once the race course has been established by the Chief Race Officer, you can take a fix using your compass to position yourself on the chart. Once you know exactly where you are, you can establish your position in relation to deep/shallow water; strong/weak tides; tidal direction; and how wind bends may affect you from surrounding land masses. This knowledge could be the difference between a gold or silver medal, and could psychologically give you more confidence to do well in the race. It is well worth doing at important national and international events. If and when you are coach-supported at an event, this will all be done for you. Your coach will have the relevant information ready to pass on to you when you arrive at the race area.

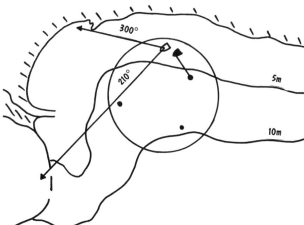

Tacking angle for the conditions

You must use your compass to work out your tacking angle for the conditions of the day. This will assist you in establishing the

Where is the mark? *Know your compass course bearings for each leg of the course.*

following key points:

- Wind direction
- Wind shifts
- Lay line calls on the beat

It is important to remember that as both wind speed and sea state change, so will your tacking angle. Generally speaking, the flatter the water, the narrower your tacking angle will be, and vice versa as the sea state increases.

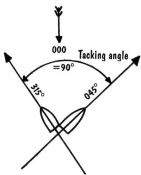

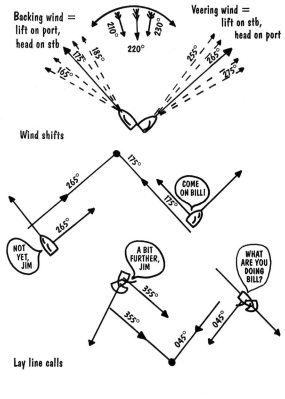

Wind shift tracking

This is an important part of pre-race preparation in order to establish the following key points:

• What is the wind direction at present in relation to the daily prediction?
• Is there an oscillating wind direction?
• Is there a steady wind direction?

Whilst in the starting area, wind shift tracking should take place for a period of at least 20 minutes to establish exactly what the wind is doing before the start. If the sea state is relatively flat, this can be done by putting the boat 'head-to-wind' and holding her there for approximately 30 seconds. If, however, the sea state is choppy, it is better to sail close-hauled on either tack; by knowing your tacking angle this will give you the wind direction. This should be done every few minutes in order to develop your wind shift tracking chart.

Knowing what the wind direction is at start time, and what it may do next as you come off the starting line, is your ace card. This could make the difference between being among the 'chocolates' at the first windward mark or not!

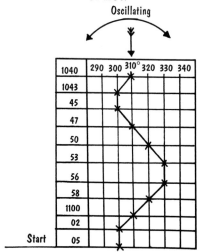

At the start time the wind is max left, lifting the port tack, and is expected to go right next

Transits

Your compass is also put to good use to establish a transit along the starting line if and when you cannot achieve a good transit with an object on the shore. With this compass bearing of the starting line you can now sail along the line confidently, allowing for any tide/surface current knowing that you are on or near the line approaching start time. Make sure that you allow a little extra safety margin should the one-minute rule be in force.

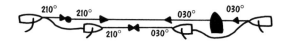

Wind shifts to windward

Sailing at a venue with an oscillating breeze, or one with a natural wind bend over the race area, is when the compass comes into its own and helps to ensure that you are going to be among the 'chocolates' at the windward mark. Having established your tacking angle during your pre-start preparations, you know what your compass headings are on both port and starboard tacks. From the data gathered from your pre-start wind shift tracking chart, you also know which tack is your freeing tack off the starting line.

Immediately after the start, your first tactical move is to ensure that you are on the lifting tack. If that is port tack, then make sure that your positioning on the start line allows you to get on to port as soon as possible having cleared the line, unless you have been able to start on port tack (very rare in the bigger fleets). Now that you are on the lifting tack and have settled down, you are looking for the expected header. While sailing on starboard tack, a minus reading indicates the header, while on port tack it is a plus reading; and as this happens, so the appropriate action is taken. If the shifts are fairly frequent, then it would be advisable to tack straight away, whereas if you thought it was heading you into a wind bend it would be better to carry on a little further to take full advantage of the bend.

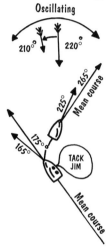

Oscillating

Wind shifts on the running leg

As you approach the windward mark, you know whether you are on a lift or a header; this tells you whether or not to bear away or gybe to start the running leg so that you are in sequence with the wind shifts downwind. Using your wind indicator, you can now detect the shifts downwind so that you are not sailing by the lee.

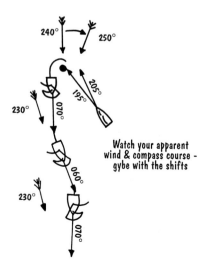

Watch your apparent wind & compass course - gybe with the shifts

Wind bends

Pre-start you will use your compass to detect a natural wind bend over the race area (these are normally found in bays). Sail the windward leg on either tack, and as you progress to windward you may see that you are either being lifted/headed steadily. This tells you that you are sailing in a wind bend created by a natural surrounding land mass.

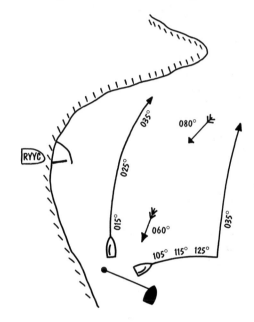

Course leg bearings

It is important for you to know the course leg bearings once the race management team have designated the windward mark bearing,

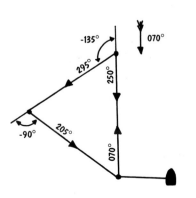

Having rounded the leeward mark, GBR must quickly assess whether she is on a lift on port tack or a header, and immediately take the appropriate action in an oscillating breeze. If she is down on her compass heading she should tack; if she is high she should stay, keeping in mind her overall strategy for the beat (weather forecast and tide/current).

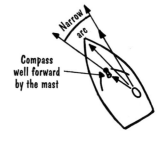

just in case visibility becomes poor during the race or the marks are not very conspicuous. Many a time I have seen the leading boat head off in the wrong direction on either the reach or running leg and others have followed!

Positioning of the compass

Only one compass is needed in the boat; this keeps down the all-up weight and expense. It should be positioned well forward in the boat to keep your angle of sight as narrow as possible between compass, telltales and waves.

Summary

As stated at the beginning of this chapter, the compass is very important; and to succeed in the sport in the future it can only be advantageous to learn how to use one. In our youth training we teach 11–12-year-olds how to use one at Optimist/Cadet level – so that the compass becomes functional in the boat and not just something to 'psych out' the opposition in the dinghy park, or something in which to keep your pet goldfish!

11

Match Racing

Watching a match race (the America's Cup, BT-sponsored youth event or whatever) quickly shows that there is much more to the contest than simply one boat racing against another. No doubt the challenge of learning new skills is part of the reason for the increasing interest in match racing, together with the lure of the international match racing scene with its huge cash prizes, or even a place on an America's Cup boat. And don't forget there is now a match racing event in the Olympic Games. There is a Senior Circuit at international level and, more recently, an International Circuit for youth sailors. Of course, these experts must learn their skills somewhere, so there is now much more activity at national level, which

The leader wants to finish as soon as possible and will already have decided whether or not to tack on DEN to win. She will only tack if she wants to protect the right hand side of the beat or if she is on a header on starboard tack. She will stay on starboard tack if she thinks the left hand side is favoured or if she is on a lift and expecting a header soon. DEN wants to make the race last longer and draw the leader into making a mistake, and so should go into a tacking dual, if possible, and keep the leader away from the lay line for the finishing line.

could eventually lead to a future America's Cup helm coming from club level.

While new skills are important – there is even an additional and separate section of the Racing Rules devoted to it – the basics of expert helmsmanship and top-level crewing are also essential. Without the ability to turn on the best boat speed when required, you may have already lost.

Match racing at club level can be organised quite easily. Any class of boat can be used (including singlehanders), and it stimulates good, exciting, close racing. This in turn sharpens up your boat handling skills as well as your overall knowledge of the Racing Rules, which can only be to your advantage in fleet racing events.

For the UK to develop future top match racers we need to establish much more training in match racing, especially for our youth sailors, so that in time they will become good senior match racers. This type of programme is exactly what was started in New Zealand some ten or fifteen years ago, and it is the reason why they are ranked number one in the world today – and have been for some time.

Getting started

Basic match race training should start under the direction of the club race training committee, RYA Race Trainers/Instructors or Racing Coaches, for anyone who wants to learn. Without doubt, it is an extremely exciting side of our sport. Enthusiasts can progress from club level to national events and, once they become successful and gain recognition, can then move up to the International Circuit.

Match racing is covered by the International Yacht Racing Rules and, in particular, Appendix B6. It is easy to organise on the water with a strong race management team, backed up by a couple of locally appointed 'on the water umpires'.

Little space is required, because usually a windward leeward course is set, above a start and finish line; both windward and leeward marks are normally left to starboard.

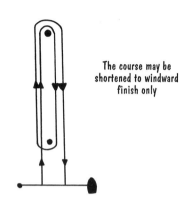

The course may be shortened to windward finish only

The format for an event requires a round-robin series where, after each yacht has raced against each other once or twice, the four winning yachts go forward to a semi-final. The two yachts that win these semi-finals then go on to the final. The two losing yachts race against each other for third place.

Starting procedure

The starting procedure for match racing is notably different from that for fleet racing, and it progresses as follows:

- 10 minutes to the start of match 1 – flag F raised and sound signal (the Attention signal).
- 6 minutes to the start of match 1 – flag F down (no sound signal).
- 5 minutes to the start of match 1 – numeral pennant 1 (or other match identifying flag) raised and sound signal (the Warning signal).
- 4 minutes to the start of match 1 – flag P (or blue shape) raised and sound signal (the preparatory signal). This signals the beginning of Entry Time, which lasts for 2

minutes; until now, each boat must have remained outside the limit of the starting line, at her designated end. Both boats must enter the starting area within the next 2 minutes (Entry Time), initially by crossing the starting line from the course side.

- 2 minutes to the start of match 1 – sound signal, but only if either boat has not yet entered the starting area (which will then incur a penalty).
- Start Time – Warning signal down and Warning signal raised for second match: 5 minutes to second start.

Of course, at club level you may just have the one match, especially in the early days of training. But if it is applicable, match 2 goes through the same procedure, followed by match 3 etc. It is usual to restrict the number to ten boats.

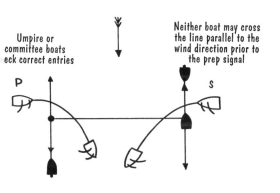

Umpire or committee boats eck correct entries

Neither boat may cross the line parallel to the wind direction prior to the prep signal

P

S

Having entered the starting area correctly and within the 2-minute period allowed, the two boats manoeuvre against each other to acquire the best start, and thereafter race the other boat around the course – creating some very close, exciting racing (keeping in mind that this is a non-contact sport!). Pre-start manoeuvres are a game of cat and mouse, with each trying to anticipate the other skipper's thoughts and trying to disguise their own plans and moves, all essentials of a good match.

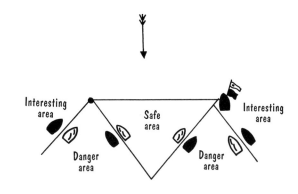

Interesting area

Safe area

Interesting area

Danger area

Danger area

All the time, you must constantly be thinking about:

- The other boat
- The 'playing area'
- The time to start
- The distance to the line
- The Racing Rules

The advice is to get into the 'play park' early, so that your opponent cannot set up a trap and either force you to delay entering beyond the time limit, and so collect a penalty, or enter on his terms. It seems particularly attractive to enter early if you are the port boat, as this might give you the chance to get across to the other end of the line – and on to starboard ready to hound your opponent.

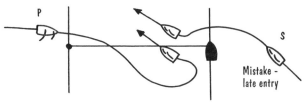

P

S

Mistake - late entry

The aim at this stage is to restrict and control the other boat's manoeuvrability. This is most easily done by following very close astern, so that should the other boat luff, you can put your bow above its quarter, denying freedom to tack; if it bears away, you can turn inside.

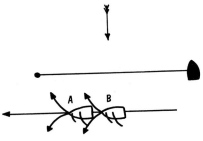

A luffs, so can B. A bears away, so can B,
to control A into the danger area

Of course, the boat ahead tries to break clear, and this is what leads to the increasingly tighter circling manoeuvres we see in all the pictures. Usually the first boat to break away loses the initiative – at that stage – and then tries to regain the upper hand. While it would be ideal always to stay between the opposition and the start line, as you would for a conventional race start, it is usually more important to try to control your opponent. Ideally, at around start time you should be in such a position that you can reach faster for the line than they can, so that you start ahead of them.

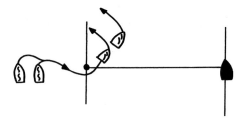

It does not matter how late you are after the start signal, but being in control at the start of the beat is crucial. To achieve this, you require:

- Good boat handling techniques.
- An excellent working knowledge of the rules
- Determination
- Controlled aggression

Combine all these qualities, and you have a good chance of becoming a successful match racer.

Pre-start manoeuvres

On entering the starting area, we now need to look at some of the most common pre-start manoeuvres for both boats. At all times keep in mind your safe zones, within which you want to say, in order not to risk being sailed out at the start.

Starboard entry boat (referred to as S)

On entering, S initially checks that she has entered correctly by observing whether the yellow flag has been lowered on the committee boat. Having done that, she quickly establishes her initial collision course with the port-entry boat. The port-tack boat is now obliged to keep clear, and must physically show to the umpires how she intends to do this – either by luffing or bearing away. S may now alter course to force the port-tack boat to take further action to keep clear, as long as she always gives the port-tack boat the avenue of escape in a seamanlike manner.

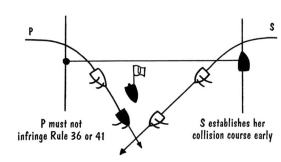

P must not
infringe Rule 36 or 41

S establishes her
collision course early

Port-entry boat (referred to as P)

Check entry by observing the blue flag. P now has two options:

    1 To pass to windward of S and into a clockwise circle.

    2 Pass across the bows of S into an anticlockwise circle.

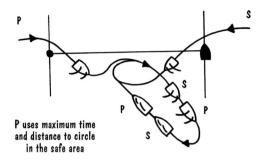

P uses maximum time
and distance to circle
in the safe area

The majority of skippers on a port-tack boat will take the first option in order to commence circling in the starboard half of the safe zone. However, if the second option is chosen, P must be able to cross the bows of S, otherwise she will be caught out under Rule 36, as S can bear away at her – constantly forcing P to gybe away if necessary, and into the danger zone.

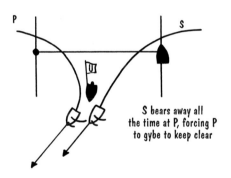

S bears away all
the time at P, forcing P
to gybe to keep clear

Most skippers will initially take a long port entry above S, and then gybe back at them below the starboard lay line for the committee boat. When S attacks P, she will normally pass to windward and gybe round below S, and then go into the gyrating cat and mouse mode. Beware: many skippers and crews become rather blasé about circling, and fall into the trap of either a boat handling mistake, leaving them dead in the water, or infringing the tacking, gybing rule (Rule 41) or port and starboard rule (Rule

36). While circling, tacticians must be fully aware of time and distance to the line for the all-critical break for the line – too early or too late could spell disaster.

P, clear ahead, must now be very careful not to infringe Rule 41. However, if the distance between them is fairly tight, her best tactic will be to bear away and gybe. As long as P clear astern has the avenue of escape across S's transom, the gybing boat is clear – and umpires would normally 'green flag' any protest from P clear astern.

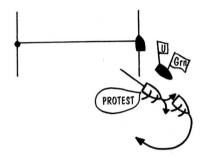

They would not, however, do so if S, clear astern and close, bears away inside P clear ahead, so that they then become overlapped and the windward boat gybes, leaving S having to make a violent alteration of course to avoid a collision if she can. So, once again, be careful.

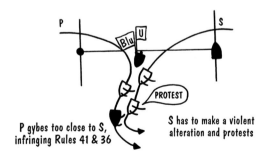

P gybes too close to S,
infringing Rules 41 & 36

S has to make a violent
alteration and protests

This is a head-to-head collision course entry when P luffs and so does S, until the eventual outcome is that they are both alongside each other head-to-wind. Boat handling skills come into good use now –

who will stall out and crack up first? Nine times out of ten it is P, who flops on to starboard tack – and so the chase begins.

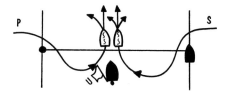

S may alter towards P as long as P has an avenue of escape. P must now be careful not to infringe Rule 41

However, it has been known for S to flop on to port tack and so P makes the chase. *Defence*: If a boat is sailed out of the safe zone it will need to look for obstructions large enough to lose the chasing boat and escape.

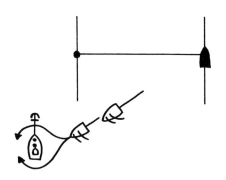

Failing that, the best manoeuvre is to go head-to-wind, gather your thoughts, and decide on your next move – at least you will be close to the opposition in this position.

Race strategy

Part of your pre-start tactics must take into account which side of the beat you want to go up, so that you can position yourself accordingly on the line in relation to the opposition. If you do not get your positioning right and thereafter, then the start is a mere formality. If you are to leeward and the left side pays – end of story!

And vice versa for the windward boat if right pays. So try very hard to be on the correct side of your opponent should this apply on the day.

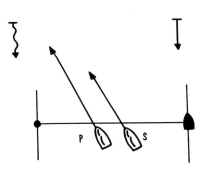

P secures the leeward slot to reach the weaker tide first

First beat

After the start, one boat will have the opportunity to take the advantage – and once she has that advantage she must be very ruthless and bury the opposition far enough behind to be able to start the run in clear wind. The golden rule, as always, is stay between the opposition and windward mark, giving them as much dirty air as possible to create a big enough gap to escape down the running leg.

S will give P maximum dirty wind for as long as possible

Running leg

As she approaches the windward mark, she will have assessed whether to bear away or gybe to get back to the leeward mark as quickly as possible. From then on, everything she does will depend on what the opposition does because she must stay between them and the next mark, keeping clear wind.

P keeping clear; wind will stay between S and the leeward mark or finish

If you are close enough to the opposition on the run, gybe at them gybe for gybe right on top of their wind to close them down, timing your attack so that you can gain the overlap at the end of the run or manage to pass them by the time you get to the finishing line; watch out for Rule 39 and your lay lines.

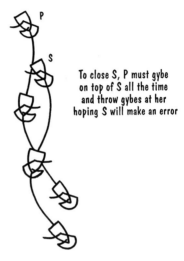

To close S, P must gybe on top of S all the time and throw gybes at her hoping S will make an error

As with all the other disciplines in our sport, practice makes perfect, so build up your training programmes for the big events. Match racing is excellent fun for both competitors and spectators.

12

Race Management

The management of racing has come a long way in recent years – as it needed to in order to give competitors exciting racing and a value-for-money service.

Over the years there have been too many mismanaged events where the competitors have come off the water disappointed with the race for a variety of reasons:

- The course itself, eg too long and boring, or not set correctly for the wind direction.
- The race committee making a wrong decision, eg abandoning a race when they should not have; letting it run out of the time limit when they could have shortened the course, etc. Of course, competitors have also been at fault, eg not reading the Sailing Instructions properly or, worse still, now knowing all the signals that may be used by the Chief Race Officer, and therefore not knowing and understanding what is going on.

Sailing instructions

All these problems are slowly but surely being overcome by producing Race Officers who are actually qualified to run races at club, regional, national and international levels of racing. Sailing Instructions have become more standardised, with local variations, and so the whole scene of race management is greatly improving – which is excellent news for the sport as a whole.

With the style of racing changing dramatically in recent years, the whole racing scene is very much upbeat for both race committees and competitors. During the early 1980s the World Youth Championships moved away from the traditional six- or seven-race event and became a ten-race event; it is now twelve-race event, giving competitors more racing and better value for money. Many class associations have since followed suit. Races last approximately 45 minutes to 1 hour, with much more mark rounding and closer, more tactical, racing. Boat handling and knowledge of the Racing Rules therefore play a more important role in racing – all good exciting stuff for competitors and spectators alike.

In 1992, at the IYRU World Youth Championships in Portugal, new-style courses were introduced as a trial for the Olympic Games in Spain the same year. These were so enjoyed by the competitors that they have been in every event since, and have been adopted by the Olympics as well as many other national and international classes. They are now also filtering through to club level and providing everyone with more exciting racing.

Competitors need to know and understand the following:

- Notice of Race and Sailing Instructions (take a copy with you if possible).
- All the signals and starting system being used by the Chief Race Officer.
- Is a tally system in and out being operated? If there is, do not forget it! If you do, it will mean disqualification – a complete waste of time, money and effort!

Signals afloat

Flag L	Flown ashore = Notice on Noticeboard. Read before going afloat.
Flag L	Flown afloat = Come within hail of CRO and/or follow me.
Answering pennant	Flown ashore/afloat = Indefinite postponement Flown above numeral pennants 1–0 = number of hours of postponement.
Answering pennant with flag A	Flown ashore or afloat = Postponed until a later date.
Answering pennant with flag H (see column opposite)	Flown afloat = Postponed – new signals ashore (all competitors return to shore immediately.
Flag G	Flown afloat by committee boat and gate launch = Gate start.
Flag Z	Flown afloat by committee boat = Fixed line start.
Class flag	Flown afloat = Warning signal at 10 minutes to start time *or* 5 minutes to start time after a general recall. Check Sailing Instructions.
Flag P	Flown afloat = Preparatory Signal at 5 minutes to start. Now under Racing Rules.

Flag I	Flown at or before Preparatory Signal = 1 minute; 'Round the Ends' rule in force. Lowered with sound signal prior to the start.
Flag X	Flown at start time = Individual recall. Flown until all boats have returned correctly or for 4 minutes. Lowered after 4 minutes even if boats are still returning, so do not think you have corrected when X comes down. It may be that 4 minutes have elapsed, but not necessarily that *you* have corrected. You may have to go further if dipping the line with no Flag I in force.
1st substitute	Flown afloat = General recall (a good friend of mine!). Used when the CRO is not happy with the start for whatever reason: unidentified boats over the line at start time, timing error, or wind shift pre-start are the most common reasons.
Flag N	Flown afloat = Race abandoned, about to be re-sailed. Return to the starting area.
Flag N above flag H	Flown afloat = Race abandoned. Return to shore as soon as possible and check Noticeboard for further instructions.
Flag S	Flown afloat = Pre-start: sail a shorter course as per Sailing Instructions. Post-start: shorten course. Finish as per Sailing Instructions or at a rounding mark between that mark and a committee boat.
Blue flag	Flown afloat = Committee boat on station as the finishing vessel. Finishing line as per Sailing Instructions.

As a competitor, it is important for you to know and understand all these signals and their implications. If necessary, stick a reference sheet of them somewhere handy on your boat. It is most dispiriting to miss out on a good result because of a lack of knowledge of these signals and the Sailing Instructions.

Any persons acting as Race Officer at *any* level must know what they are doing, as must their team. They must also have a knowledge of the capabilities and limitations of the boats and sailors for whom they are catering. They must know what is the maximum wind strength and sea state that the majority of the fleet can handle. Safety and the welfare of the fleet must always be the main consideration, ensuring that there is sufficient safety cover at all times.

Many Race Officers in the past have been pressurised by competitors to allow racing, or not to allow racing, because of too much wind or lack of it. This must not be allowed. The CRO must make the decision 'to race or not to race' based on all the facts available to him or her at the time. The CRO's decision is then final and should be respected.

Race Officer courses are available at club and open meeting levels. If you are interested, contact your Regional Race Management Co-ordinator for details of courses in your area. Useful books available from the Royal Yachting Association are: *Club Race Officers' Handbook* and *The Race Management Book*.

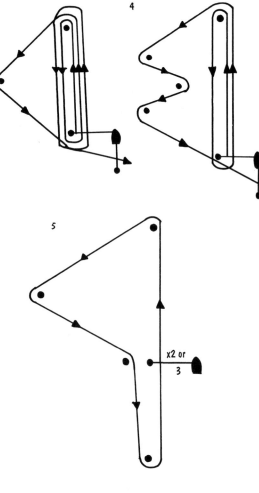

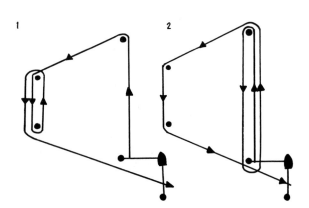

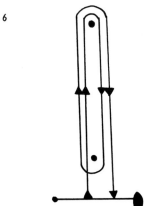

13

RYA National Race Training Scheme

As in any sport, at whatever level – whether it be club champion or World Champion – you must train if you want to win.

The RYA National Race Training Scheme began in 1977 and is for everyone – youth and adult in any class of boat. Race training is available through various channels. Your personal requirements and your present standard, and also what you wish to achieve, all have a bearing on what type of training you should adopt:

- Self training/coaching
- Club race training
- Class association race training
- Regional Squad training
- National Squad training
- International Team training

Within the UK, race training at club, regional and national level is taken care of by the RYA Race Training Committee. It is the RYA's policy that every racing-oriented club should have its own Race Trainer/Instructor or Racing Coach to provide race training for the club members, both youths and adults. Race training at club level is normally broken down into three areas:

- Youth race training
- Adult race training
- Specific class training

RYA Race Trainers/Instructors

Any club wishing to have a Club Race Trainer/Instructor can nominate a person for a two-day course organised by their Regional Race Training Co-ordinator. The nominated person must be a racing sailor with at least five years' experience at open meeting and national level of competition. They must also hold a first aid certificate and, if intending to use a coach boat, a Level Four powerboating certificate.

It is essential that the appointed Race Trainer/Instructor organises at least one, if not two, Race Training Seminars during the year as required by the members. This raises the standard of racing within the club which, in turn, filters through to regional and national level. It is satisfying to see that many clubs are now involved in this scheme.

Club Race Training Seminar

Seminars can be organised with the help of the RYA Regional Race Training Co-ordinator, if his assistance is required. One of the RYA Racing Coaches will be invited to run the seminar, which will cover a variety of subjects as required by the membership. This programme is normally conducted over a weekend – 0930 Saturday until 1600 Sunday. Two-thirds of the seminar will normally be spent afloat doing practical race training exercises, and the remainder of the time is spent on lectures on racing topics with videos and debriefs of the day's practical work. A Club Race Training Seminar would take the following format:

Saturday
0930–1030 – Introduction, Discussion, Briefing
1030–1230 – *Afloat*: Individual racing: course No 1
1230–1300 – Debrief, Discussion, Video
1300–1345 – Lunch
1345–1400 – Briefing
1400–1600 – *Afloat*: Boat handling exercises 1, 2, 4, 7, 8
1600–1700 – De-rig, Discussion, Video

Sunday
0930–1030 – Lecture (as required)
1030–1300 – *Afloat*: Starting practice: exercises 9, 10, 11, Individual Racing: course No 2
1300–1345 – Lunch
1345–1500 – Briefing. *Afloat*: Individual racing: courses Nos 1–5 as required
1500–1530 – De-rig and change
1530–1600 – Debrief, Discussion, Video
1600   Depart

On completion of a successful Club Race Training Seminar you should have achieved two things:

  1 You should have enjoyed yourself!

  2 You should have learned enough to improve your own personal performance within the sport, and also to want this to be an annual fixture at your club.

Any club wishing to organise a Club Race Training Seminar can obtain the name and telephone number of their Regional Race Training Co-ordinator by contacting their RYA Regional Executive or the Racing Division at RYA Headquarters.

RYA Racing Coaches

These are nominated by class association committees. Anyone wishing to be an RYA Racing Coach must be recommended to the RYA Racing Division for their consideration. All applications are checked by the RYA coaching staff and suitable applicants are invited to attend the annual Racing Coaches Course, which is normally held in November. Those entrants who pass this course are then qualified to run Race Training Courses or Seminars at club, regional and national level, and can also look after UK teams at international events.

Any club or class association requiring the assistance of a Racing Coach can get names and addresses from their Regional Race Training Co-ordinator or RYA Headquarters.

Regional Race Training Co-ordinators

There are 13 Regional Race Training Co-ordinators covering all the RYA regions, and they are responsible to the RYA Senior National Racing Coach for organising and co-ordinating race training at club and regional level. Regional Race Training Co-ordinators are appointed by the RYA Racing Division in consultation with the appropriate Regional Chairman. Any club requiring advice and assistance on any aspect of race training should contact the Co-ordinator in their region.

RYA Staff Coaches

The Staff Coaches come under the direction of the RYA Race Training Committee and the RYA Racing Manager. They cover all aspects of race training at all levels: clubs; class associations; regions; national teams; international events and Olympic teams. There are four staff coaches covering all aspects of racing and classes of boats, and any club or class association requiring the assistance of one of these coaches can contact them at RYA Headquarters.

UK Youth Scheme

Over the years, this scheme has gone from strength to strength. The RYA Youth Policy is reviewed by the RYA Race Training Committee every five years, the next review being 1998. The following classes have their own coach, coach boat and coaching equipment supplied by the Eric Twiname Trust Fund together with RYA and Sports Council funding.

Initially, youngsters obtain race training through their club's Race Trainer/Instructor, advancing through the RYA badge scheme. There are three levels of race training courses: Introductory, Intermediate and Advanced. Youngsters participating in these courses will receive a red badge after completing the Introductory course, a white badge after the Intermediate course, and a blue badge for Advanced level. Race Trainers/Instructors are qualified to run the Introductory and Intermediate courses, but the Advanced course has to be run by an RYA Racing Coach.

Introductory Race Training Course

DAY 1	Course intro, Safety & Programme	*Lecture*: Introduction to racing How to prepare – Starting procedure *Afloat*: practice course 1	L	*Lecture*: Boat handling – tacking & gybing *Afloat*: practice Exercises 4, 7, 8	Debrief Discussion Video	*Lecture*: Race management Visual signals
DAY 2	*Lecture*: Starting techniques	*Afloat*: Starting practice exercises 9–11	U	*Afloat*: Boat handling practice exercises 4, 7, 8 o/c race course 2	Debrief Discussion Video	*Lecture*: Basic Racing Rules
DAY 3	*Lecture*: Basic boat tuning	*Afloat*: Boat tuning serial exercise 12	N	*Afloat*: Boat handling practice exercises 4, 13, 14 o/c race course 3	Debrief Discussion Video	Free
DAY 4	*Lecture*: Basic race strategy	*Afloat*: Practical race strategy assessment o/c race course 4	C	*Afloat*: Team racing exercise 3	Debrief Discussion Video	*Lecture*: Tactics
DAY 5	*Lecture*: Protest procedures	*Afloat*: Match racing course 6	H	*Afloat*: Racing course 1	Debrief Discussion	Depart

Intermediate Race Training Course

D A Y 1	Course intro, Safety & Programme	*Lecture:* Self preparation o/c afloat racing course 1	L	*Afloat:* Boat handling exercises 4, 7, 8	Debrief Discussion Video	*Lecture:* Boat preparation & Rule 20
D A Y 2	*Lecture:* Boat handling techniques	*Afloat:* Boat handling exercises 5 & 10	U	*Afloat:* Continue boat handling exercises 4 & 10 o/c race course 2	Debrief Discussion Video	*Lecture:* Race management
D A Y 3	*Lecture:* Starting techniques	*Afloat:* Starting practice exercises 9 & 11 o/c race course 3	N	*Afloat:* Continue starting practice o/c race course 4	Debrief Discussion Video	*Lecture:* Racing rules
D A Y 4	*Lecture:* Boat tuning	*Afloat:* Boat tuning exercise 12 o/c race course 5	C	*Afloat:* Team racing 2 v 2 exercise 3	Debrief Discussion Video	*Lecture:* Protest Procedures
D A Y 5	*Lecture:* Compass work	*Afloat:* Use of compass: line bias – wind shift tracking – course bearings use of wind shifts	H	*Afloat:* Racing course 1 & 2	Debrief Discussion	Depart

Advanced Race Training Course

Course intro Safety & Programme	*Lecture:* Championship preparations	*Afloat:* Racing course 1 o/c boat handling exercises 4, 5, 6	L	*Afloat:* Boat handling Exercises 7, 8, 10 o/c race course 2	Debrief Discussion Video	*Lecture:* Physical fitness & training
0730–0800 P.T. o/c Breakfast	*Lecture:* Race strategy & meteorology	*Afloat:* Starting techniques exercises 9 & 11	U	*Afloat:* Group training o/c race course 3	Debrief Discussion Video	*Lecture:* Racing Rules
	Lecture: Tactics	*Afloat:* Team racing 2 v 2 exercise 3	N	*Afloat:* Match racing o/c racing – race course 4	Debrief Discussion Video	*Lecture:* Protest procedure & hearing
	Lecture: Boat tuning	*Afloat:* Boat tuning serial o/c race course 5	C	*Afloat:* Group training o/c race course 1	Debrief Discussion Video	*Lecture:* Wind strategy
	Lecture: Race management	*Afloat:* Group training	H	*Afloat:* Race course 2	Debrief Discussion	Depart

As their skills improve, youngsters progress up their specific class ranking ladder by attending open meetings and national championships until they are in their class association's national squad. Once in their respective squads they get specific training and attention from their class coaches. Which route a youngster takes through the Youth Training Scheme depends very much on bodyweight and strength as well as age.

Over the past 17 years, most of the top youngsters have started in either Optimists, Mirrors or Cadets, moving up at the age of 15 to the 420s, Laser Radial or Laser 1. They are then involved at the senior end of the Youth Scheme for a three-year period before moving into the Olympic Programme in the 470, Laser 1 or Finn. Using this system, the Youth Scheme has produced 26 World Champions, 16 European Champions and 2 pre-Olympic gold medallists. In 1994, past and present Youth Squad members won 11 gold medals, 3 silver medals and 1 bronze medal – and with good talent continuing to come through the system, the future looks rosy. Our problem is how to hang on to this success. This is where the Race Trainers/Instructors are invaluable by feeding the system from club level. Long may it continue!

National Youth Squad

Over the years, the National Youth Squad has been formed to give continuation training prior to the UK Youth Championships and trials to select youngsters for the various international events such as the World Youth Championships, Kiel Week, Youth Spa Regatta and, in conjunction with their class associations and coaches, the Laser 1 Youth Europeans and the 420 Youth Europeans.

The RYA organises three weekends at the end of each year (usually two in November and one in December) for training and selection into the National Youth Squad in

420, Laser 1 and Laser Radials for the following spring. These weekends are open to youngsters who are recommended by Regional Race Training Co-ordinators and RYA Race Training Coaches. From these weekend trials, twenty 420s, twenty Laser 1s, and twelve Laser Radials are chosen to go into the National Youth Squad for continuation training during March and early April. From there they can enter the UK Youth Championships, which are normally held during the Easter holidays, and go on to the selection trials for the World Youth Championships and the other international events as mentioned previously, which are usually held in the summer of that year. If the World Youth Championships are to be held in the Southern Hemisphere in the December or January, then the selection is normally not made until the school half-term holiday in the autumn. The selected teams continue with regular training regimes built around their educational programme, with financial support given by the RYA/Sports Council.

Any youngsters or parents wanting further information on the UK Youth Scheme should contact the RYA Racing Division at RYA Headquarters in Eastleigh.

Youth match racing

We have recently begun to look more seriously at youth match race training and youth match racing events because of the results and level of competition in this discipline emerging from other countries. For the UK to be successful in match racing in the future, both on the Senior Circuit and at Olympic level, we must train our youth. Youth match race training is now beginning to take place at regional and national level, with a UK Youth Match Racing Championship being held each summer. The winners of this event then go on to the International Youth Match Racing

Championship held in Auckland, New Zealand, in November of each year.

Since the conception of this championship in 1990, we have finished fourth, fourth, third, second and first in 1994. Ten teams are invited to attend this prestigious event, and it is an excellent opportunity for our youngsters to develop their match racing skills for the future. Ben Vines is a good example – he won the silver medal in New Zealand in 1992 and then went on to win the BT Senior Match Racing Nationals in 1994.

Youngsters wishing to be involved in the RYA Youth Match Racing Programme should contact their Regional Race Training Co-ordinator.

14

Race Training Exercises

Exercises 1–14

Exercise 1

This is used to bring out the following aspects of the sport: boat handling, starting, tactics, rules, mark rounding and sail trim.

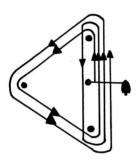

Exercise 2

This is used to improve on gybing skills and mark-rounding techniques; and also starting, tactics and the Racing Rules.

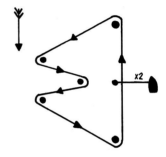

Good boat balance and trim equal maximum power and speed. Perfection!

Exercise 3

This is a good exercise for team racing practice, and improves boat handling skills, rules and tactics.

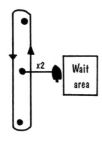

Exercise 4

Boat handling exercise: Five tacks on the beat. In spinnaker boats, hoist at the top-left corner, three to five gybes, and drop at the bottom-left corner. This exercise is used only for practice and not as a race, but the Racing Rules still apply between boats. The coach boat can be anchored in the middle of the square, enabling boats to go alongside to discuss any boat handling problems. Or it can be mobile as required, for video work, etc.

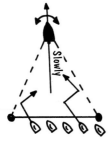

Exercise 5

This exercise is used to improve: boat handling skills, tactics and rules. Boats must stay within the triangle and leave the coach boat to either port or starboard as required by the coach.

Exercise 6

A running start to overcome problems with rounding the leeward mark in a group. Use of Rule 42 and slowing down to gain the advantage, inside a raft. If possible, have a video camera at the two boat length radius circle to prove *overlaps* or *clear ahead* and *astern*.

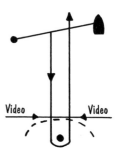

Exercise 7

Follow the leader: A good boat handling exercise in beam reaching, tacking and gybing. It is also useful for keeping warm when it is cold or for warming up if you are already cold. Tighten up the tacks at the apex of the windward session, and likewise the gybes near the end of the run.

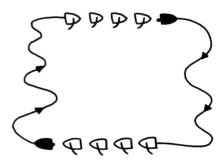

Exercise 8

Good for boat handling skills, this exercise goes as follows:

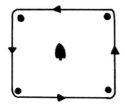

- Beam reach 'whistle' – close-hauled.
  Subsequent 'whistles' – tack
  simultaneously.
- Beam reach 'whistle' – turn on to a dead
  run (spinnaker boats hoist spinnakers).
  Subsequent 'whistles' – all gybe
  simultaneously.
- Beam reach and repeat the exercise if
  required.

Exercise 10

A good exercise for: starting, boat handling
skills, tactics, rules and mark rounding. This
exercise is normally run under racing
conditions, thus putting participants under
even more pressure!

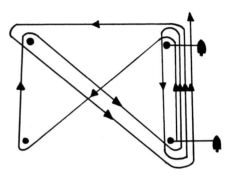

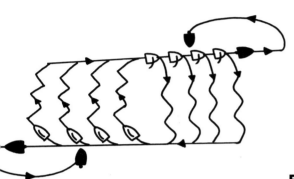

Exercise 9

Boxed start for starting practice in a
crowded area, like starts at major events. It
is followed by a short windward leg, leaving
the mark to port and rounding the leeward
mark to port to finish, for leeward mark-
rounding practice. In order to work on boat
handling skills at the same time, coaches
can set a certain amount of tacks and gybes
during this exercise. All boats must be in the
box before commencing starting procedure;
they must now keep their eyes open for the
Racing Rules: *no contact*.

Exercise 11

Mobile start line: After starting, the line
moves to windward with the competitors
who must stay between the imaginary line
both ahead and astern of the coach boats
until they get to the lay lines for the mark.
The same now applies on the running leg
back to the starting area. As the coach boats
progress to windward, they also close each
other – thus making it tighter for the sailors.

This is a good exercise for a group of up to
approximately 20 dinghies or 12 yachts.

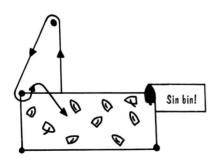

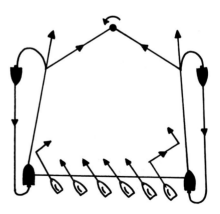

Whilst running in light airs both helm and crew should sit further forward and heel the boat more to windward to reduce both the wetted area and surface drag. It is faster!

Boat balance is a little too much to leeward. Ideally the helm could be a little lower on the wire and ease the main a little and/or ease the kicker slightly if overpowered.

*More people on board means more chaos!
Everyone must know his/her specific job and
stick to it. Practise and training makes perfect.*

Exercise 12

Boat tuning: One boat sets up for maximum
speed and pointing ability for the
conditions, and the other is allowed to
adjust controls. Commence the leg until it is
obvious that one boat is either going faster
and/or pointing higher, then stop. Make an
adjustment as required, and go again to see
the difference. Stop, adjust again, go again,
stop, adjust, go again and stop. Tack and
repeat the procedure to the windward limit
area, then on opposite tacks return
downwind. Discuss achievements, exchange
information and ideas to the leeward area,

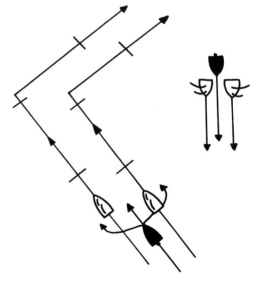

swap positions and roles, and then repeat the exercise. Ideally, on the third test, boats should be swapped to enable the participants to get a feel for each other's boats and to look at their own from the outside. Participants can also watch from the coach boat while a third party sails their craft. A great deal can be gained from such an effective boat tuning session. Working with a colleague of equal calibre is the best way to go faster and higher in all conditions.

Exercise 14

Beam reaching: Looking at sail trim, kicker tension, boat balance and trim.

Exercise 13

Tacking and gybing: Sailing around the coach boat practising roll tacks and gybes while coach videos hands and feet to establish if there are any problems.

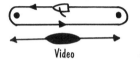

Video

The smile says it all! End of a campaign: gold medals: a job well done.

Appendix 1

Boat Tuning Log

This Boat Tuning Log should be completed after every race or race training session for your own evaluation and calibration to ensure that your faster rig settings can be recalled easily as and when they are required.

Boat Tuning Log

Date		Sea state		Sail(s) used	
Venue		Wind speed		Foils used	

RIG TENSION =

	Beating	Reaching	Running	
Mast rake				Comments
Spreader length				
Spreader angle				
Mast ram				
Kicker				
Cunningham				
Clew outhaul				
Barber hauler				
Taveller				
Jib halyard tension				
Main halyard tension				
Centreboard position				

Appendix 2

Race Analysis
What did I/we not do?

1 Technology
Hull, spars, sails, foils, fittings: are they good
  enough?

2 Boat preparation
Did anything break? Does everything work?

3 Self preparation
Am I/we fit enough – physically and
  mentally?
Physical fitness – breeds confidence
Mental fitness – breeds confidence

4 Geographical, tidal, meteorological preparation
Did I/we check for any permanent wind
  bends over the racing area due to
  surrounding land mass?
Did I/we know the strength and direction
  of any surface current throughout the
  race period over the whole of the
  course?
Did I/we have the latest weather
  information and know what the wind was
  expected to do?

5 Boat handling
Is our tacking good enough?
Is our gybing good enough (with/without
  spinnaker)?
Is our spinnaker drill quick enough?
Are we balancing the boat correctly on all
  points of sailing?
Are we trimming the boat correctly on all
  points of sailing?
Are we in full control of the boat in all
conditions and appreciate its handling
  characteristics?

6 Boat tuning
Was the rig set up correctly for the
  conditions of the day?
Was the rig tension correct?
Was the mast rake correct?
Were the spreaders the correct length and
  angle?
Was the cunningham hole tension correct
  on all points of sailing?
Was the ram set correctly?
Did we have the correct amount of mast
  bend for the conditions?
Is the mast heel in the correct position?
Is it a tight fit (no twist)?
Was the kicking strap tension correct for all
  points of sailing?
Was the traveller in the correct position for
  all points of sailing?
Did I use the mainclew outhaul correctly on
  all points of sailing?
Did I use the barber hauler system
  correctly?
Was the slot shape correct?

7 Starting
Fixed line
Did I/we select the correct end to start
  from?
Did I/we check on a transit after
  preparatory signal?
Was I up near the line at start time going at
  speed in clear wind?

Was my final approach to the line tactically correct (no one immediately to leeward of me)?

Was I on the correct tack off the line (shifty conditions)?

Did I infringe any Racing Rules?

Gate starting

Did I/we assess speed of the pathfinder?

Did I/we assess wind and tide to go early, middle or late? (also check relevant clauses from *fixed line* starting)

Did I concentrate on speed and pointing initially after starting to get away from the opposition?

8 Tactics

Did I/we take the tack closest to windward mark?

Did I/we take the tack to a nearby shoreline (if applicable) first?

Did I stay with the main bunch of the fleet?

Did I use the wind shifts/gusts/bends to advantage?

Did I get to lay line too early?

Was I always between the main bunch of the fleet and the next mark?

On the reaching legs, did I get above, on or below the rhumb line or a backing or veering wind to gain the advantage defending our wind?

On the running leg, did we get left, right or on rhumb line for above reasons?

Did I use my wind indicator to ensure I was on the correct tack, not sailing by the lee.

Was I on the correct tack during final approach to leeward mark?

Did we go for the correct end of the finishing line?

Did I use my compass correctly throughout the race?

9 Racing Rules

Did I use the Racing Rules to my advantage both as my attacking and defensive weapon?

Do I know the Racing Rules? In particular, 31 to 46 and 54?

Am I fully conversant with protest procedures?

10 Sailing instructions

Did I/we read these thoroughly?

Did we take a copy afloat with us?

Did I understand them fully?

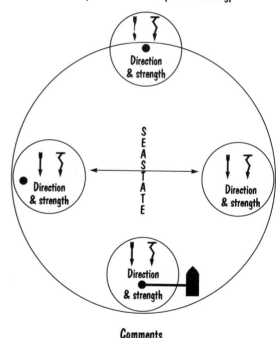

Pre & post start race analysis and strategy

Comments

Appendix 3

Coach/Competitor Communication

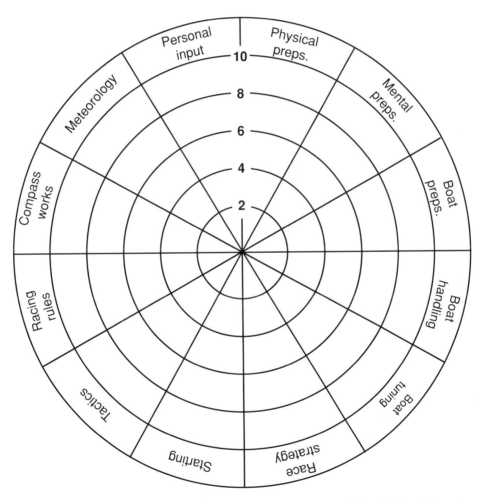

Personal Assessment presented to your coach prior to training

Score yourself 0–10 by filling in segments – re-assess with your coach periodically.

Index